LITERACY LESSONS TO HELP KIDS GET FIT & HEALTHY

Michael F. Opitz

with Jennifer Davis-Duerr

SCHOLASTIC

New York · Toronto · London · Auckland · Sydney
Mexico City · New Delhi · Hong Kong · Buenos Aires

To the health and well-being of all children.
—MFO

To Ellie, my constant source of inspiration.
—JDD

Editor: Lois Bridges
Copy and production editor: Danny Miller
Cover design: Jorge J. Namerow
Interior design: Sydney Wright

ISBN-13: 978-0-545-16324-8
ISBN-10: 0-545-16324-2

Copyright © 2010 by Michael F. Opitz
All rights reserved. Published by Scholastic Inc.
Printed in the U.S.A.

3 4 5 6 7 8 9 10   23   17 16 15 14 13 12 11 10

Contents

Acknowledgments

Although this book bears my name, it was a group effort. Countless individuals who knew of my interest in this topic sent me articles, books, and even newscasts over the eight years since I first became interested in the topic. I am greatly indebted to all and wish to acknowledge them.

Lois Bridges, editor extraordinaire, is first on the list. From the very start, Lois saw a need for the book and was patient enough to wait for me to put it together. A fitness advocate herself, she was constantly sending me new information and helpful insights, as well as encouragement, cheering, and her infamous editorial touches (i.e., the Bridges Touch) that brought clarity to the book.

Donald Graves is next on my list, for it was he who read the original introduction and first chapter several years ago. His insights, coupled with questions, led to my increased thinking and understanding about how to best present the information.

I thank my colleagues at the University of Northern Colorado: doctoral candidate Jennifer Davis-Duerr for her many contributions to this text, her copious attention to detail, and her dedication to writing the best book possible; Susan Thompson for reading and responding to the original introduction and first chapter several years ago; James A. Erekson for sending me the broadcast that I was able to use in the introduction of this text; Lindsey M. Guccione for reading and commenting on nearly every chapter; Jenni Harding-DeKam and Todd DeKam for reviewing and responding to the grid shown in Chapter 1; Alexander Sidorkin for encouraging me to apply for a sabbatical and advocating for my application, which afforded me the time to write this book in the most thoughtful manner possible. He and his son Gleb also brainstormed titles that led to the FitLit logo.

Michael P. Ford, University of Wisconsin, Oshkosh, is a friend and colleague who gave me the book about Charles Atlas that appears in one of the lessons. He also sent articles as he discovered them and listened to me talk through the overall structure of the book.

Several teachers deserve acknowledgment. Middle school health teacher Janette McCann read drafts and offered her perspective; Heidi-Jo Reyes and Ashley Montoya-Aragon, two former students who have now been teaching for five years, did the original sorting of the children's literature selections; physical education teacher and coach Stephen Guccione read and responded to much of the book. My former personal fitness trainer Doug Resh provided a wealth of information and responded to the original first chapter.

My thanks extend to Danny Miller, the meticulous copy and production editor, who brought clarity and style to this text; to Sydney Wright for her inspired design; and to all the extraordinary individuals at Scholastic.

Finally, I thank Sheryl Opitz, my wife, for her support and for keeping watch in the media and clipping newspaper articles focused on children's health issues. To all, my deepest thanks.

—*Michael F. Opitz*

I thank Dr. Michael Opitz for inviting me to take part in such a significant endeavor. Your great perseverance and creativity at the heart of this project, along with profound faith, encouragement, and support fundamental to writing partnerships, will forever serve as guiding inspirations. I also thank the many friends and family who've offered their support through unending patience, understanding, and optimism.

—*Jennifer Davis-Duerr*

Introduction

"Oh, Michael! This is big! The problem is so complex, as your writing well shows! But how are you going to tackle this issue so that teachers will feel comfortable enough with the topic so that they will devote instructional time to it?"

Such were the comments of Donald Graves, who called to give me his responses to an introduction and opening chapter I had written for a book about integrating physical fitness and reading as a way to help with the childhood obesity problem. He didn't say anything I hadn't already thought. The idea of stepping up as a reading educator to do something to help children ward off obesity and its accompanying ailments was at times overwhelming and paralyzing. In fact, after listening to what he had to offer, I decided that the topic was too challenging. I shelved it—well, sort of. Although I turned my attention to other reading-related topics, I continued to read and collect references pertaining to fitness and childhood obesity, all in an effort to more fully understand the issues and figure out what, if anything, I might be able to do to help address the problem. Called to action, how should I respond?

Fast-forward six years to February 19, 2009. I'm listening to an interview of childhood obesity expert Dr. Reggie Washington, chief medical officer of Rocky Mountain Hospital for Children, in Denver, Colorado. Among his many comments is his explanation of what he calls the No FAT Child Left Behind Act. He notes that because school district personnel feel so pressured to meet testing mandates, they have either decreased or totally eliminated recess and physical education. He makes perfectly clear that schools alone cannot solve the problem of childhood obesity but that they can help children who are living in an "obesigenic environment," an environment that simultaneously promotes eating and a sedentary lifestyle. He concludes, "This problem is so complex!"

His closing words echo Donald Graves's comments six years earlier. However, this time I find them liberating rather than paralyzing. Buoyed by all the newer evidence I have collected over the past eight years when I started drafting ideas, I am ready to present some practical ways to address the problem in manageable ways that fit into existing classroom routines. My goal is to show teachers how to help children read well to be fit.

What does it mean to read well and what does it mean to be fit? I begin Chapter 1 by answering these basic questions. I then describe the reciprocal nature of the two and explain why taking on childhood obesity and its accompanying ailments within the school day is necessary and advantageous for teachers and students alike. Next, I propose integrated instruction, a tried-and-true teaching technique, as one way to help address this burgeoning childhood health problem. Participating in integrated instruction helps learners develop deeper understandings of the topics at hand, in this case literacy and physical fitness. Ultimately, the goal is to help children discover that they can and must take charge of their own health and how they can do just that.

Also, using integrated instruction helps teachers address a variety of topics within a school day that suffers from its own form of obesity—curriculum obesity. Clearly, integrating topics such as reading and fitness is crucial for, as Wechsler, McKenna, Lee, and Dietz (2004, p. 4) note, "Health and success in school are interrelated."

Fortunately, there are specific content reading-literacy teaching strategies that can be integrated with the different components of physical fitness. They form the content of Chapters 2–5. I open each chapter with an explanation of the fitness category the chapter showcases. I then provide five content-reading teaching strategies designed to help learners use literacy (reading, writing, listening, speaking, and viewing) to acquire a deeper understanding of physical fitness concepts. Each strategy includes a title, a brief description, suggested texts (FitLit), teaching procedures, a scenario of a classroom fitness connection that shows how the teaching strategy and a specific fitness skill are integrated, and some related Web sites. I also offer lesson extensions. Finally, for those teachers who are fortunate to work closely with other professionals, I offer a Professional Collaborating Tip for each strategy.

Although chapters 2–5 are written as stand-alone chapters, keep in mind that many of the content literacy strategies serve all fitness categories. Prediction Guide, for example, is showcased in Chapter 2 as a way to help children better understand how heart rate connects to their overall physical fitness, but it can be used to teach other areas of fitness, too. In other words, I present the strategies as one way to help teachers feel self-confident about teaching reading and fitness simultaneously; there is some overlap and I encourage teachers to use the strategies in ways that are best suited to the needs of their students.

As you read Chapters 2–5, please keep in mind these two additional points:

1. The literacy lessons can easily fit into your existing classroom routines. As written, many of the lessons follow a gradual-release model of instruction in which the teacher begins with the whole class and demonstrates the expected learning. Students then work in small groups with teacher guidance and come back as a whole group to discuss their learning.

2. The lessons help students at all elementary grade levels to comprehend expository and narrative texts. Nonetheless, picture books take center stage for three reasons. First, the pictures help students with limited background understand the printed text. Second, authors use content-specific words to explain ideas enabling students to acquire new vocabulary in a meaningful context. Third, the information is less overwhelming than textbooks, enabling students to focus on a specific topic and leaving them with feelings of reading success.

Beyond the five chapters, you'll find two appendices. Appendix A provides some additional recently published children's literature selections (FitLit) that can be used for each area of fitness. The lists are intended to extend children's reading of various fitness areas. You are likely to find additional titles to add to these lists. Appendix B provides reproducibles that coincide with some of the lessons in this text.

Donald Graves was correct. How to address all areas of physical fitness within the school day to help ward off childhood obesity is multifaceted! I wholeheartedly agree with Wechsler et al. (2004, 6) who note that "Schools cannot solve the obesity epidemic on their own, but it is unlikely to be halted without strong school-based policies and programs."

Admittedly, I am a reading educator by profession, with a personal fitness-training avocation. Coming at this child health problem from a reading angle is natural for me. I make no claim to have all of the answers to this complex problem. My hope is that I have engendered enough awareness and understanding, fortified by plenty of instructional know-how, that you will feel compelled to join me in my call to action. Society in general, and children in particular, will be all the better for our efforts. Let's do it!

CHAPTER 1

Understanding
READING WELL TO BE FIT

Jocks are dumb and smart people are weak. Don't believe me? Take a look at the many advertisements that reinforce this message to children and adults alike. Just last evening I saw a television commercial that showed a muscle-clad high school boy leaving his personal trainer at the gym to get tutoring in English from what appeared to be an out-of-shape, frumpy male seated at a book-laden table in the library. This type of advertisement contributes to many misunderstandings about fitness and academics. Rather than helping children to understand that both reading and physical fitness require thinking and meaningful practice, these advertisements lead children to believe that one is either hooked on physical fitness or hooked on academics. One cannot be hooked on both. Is it any wonder that those who choose academics also often choose a sedentary lifestyle, which is one contributor of childhood obesity (Welk and Blair, 2000)?

Advertisements alone are not the problem. As childhood obesity expert Dr. Reggie Washington notes, children live in an *obesigenic environment*, which he defines as an environment that sees a decrease in physical activity both in and out of school and the proliferation of snack foods that have little or no nutritional value (i.e., junk foods). His solution includes making people aware of issues that surround childhood obesity and focusing on prevention.

And what better way to promote both awareness and prevention than by education? Change occurs from the inside out. Therefore when children perceive reading and fitness to be less about essential contributors to a healthy lifestyle and more about choosing one over the other, our goal is to help them realize this is a false dichotomy. Helping children understand the essential nature of healthy living is the aim of this book. Each activity in the book is designed to help children understand that living a healthy lifestyle is their choice and that they can take control of their health. Before looking at the activities, though, let's first take a look at my definitions of reading and fitness, as both provide the necessary grounding for this text.

What Do I Mean by "Reading Well"?

There are many theories about how children learn to read. Some propose that children first need to crack the printed code and that when they do so successfully, they are *reading well*. Others note that children must focus on meaning while reading, even as they "crack the code," because without meaning, there is no real reading. For these individuals, *reading well* means reading with comprehension. Still others note that proficient readers are those who not only can break the code and comprehend, but also read a variety of texts for specific purposes and come to the text with a questioning mind. They read with a critical stance, therefore they are *reading well*.

My definition of *reading well* draws on these different perspectives (see Figure 1.1). One needs to be able to use a variety of skills and strategies to be a proficient reader. Yet these alone are not enough, especially in this digital age of information bombardment replete with implied messages about what's hot and what's not. Children also need to be taught how to take a critical look at what they see and hear if they are to be knowledgeable, savvy consumers. For me, then, readers who are *reading well* do the following:

1. *Comprehend.* Comprehension is the heart of reading, and readers bring their background to the text in order to create meaning. That is, the readers' thoughts interact with those in the text. The result of this interaction is the creation of meaning. As readers build meaning, they use a variety of strategies. For example, they establish a purpose for reading the text and make decisions about how to read it to achieve their purpose. They might read selectively, deciding which parts need to be read more slowly or more quickly depending on their background knowledge for the text. Readers also use *pragmatics* (i.e., the context in which they are reading) and the type of reading material to guide how they read. For instance, when studying, reading might necessitate sitting at a table in a designated place. To be sure, those who are *reading well* are active, thoughtful, strategic readers (Duke and Pearson, 2001).

2. *Think about their thinking (metacognition).* Readers who are *reading well* are aware of their thought processes when reading; they are metacognitive. Therefore, they recognize

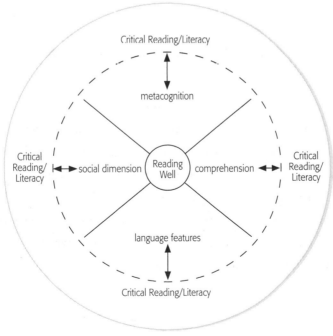

▶ Figure 1.1 *Reading Well Model*

when comprehension breaks down and what to do to restore it. If the problem is not knowing the meaning of a word, for example, readers may decide to continue reading to see if the coming text will clarify the meaning. At other times, they realize that they were not totally concentrating when reading a given passage and decide to reread.

3. **Socialize.** The ability to make personal connections not only with the characters in texts but also with other readers is an important ingredient of reading. Simply stated, readers talk about what they have read. Evidence of readers talking during reading can be found in the notes that they make to themselves in the margins of the text or on another piece of paper when reading. Discussing their discoveries and understandings with others after reading is proof enough that the social network is alive and well.

4. **Use language features.** Readers are constantly asking themselves three questions as they read: "Does this make sense?" "Does this sound right?" "Does this look right?" These three questions are an indication that readers are intuitively using three linguistic cueing systems as they read: semantic, syntactic, and graphophonic. They derive semantic cues from the text's meaning, syntactic cues from the text's grammatical structure, and graphophonic cues from sound/symbol relationships and patterns. All of these work together to help readers construct meaning.

5. **Read critically.** Critical reading is "reading in which a questioning attitude, logical analysis, and inference are used to judge the worth of text according to an established standard" (Harris and Hodges, 1995, p. 47). As the definition suggests, judgment is anything but a mere opinion. Instead, readers have some external or internal standards that help them form their judgments. For instance, they might have additional information about the given topic, which they use to compare to the current text. Critical reading calls on readers to suspend their judgments while they consider several viewpoints. It calls on readers to go beyond any one text to form their own opinions about what they have read.

Beyond *critical reading* is *critical literacy*. Critical literacy is more encompassing than critical reading in that it is, according to Jones (2006, p. 65), "an understanding that

Literacy Lessons to Help Kids Get Fit & Healthy

language practices and texts are always informed by ideological beliefs and perspectives, whether conscious or otherwise." When they are taught critical literacy, then, children are taught how to "read across the grain" (McLaughlin and DeVoogd, 2004, p. 4). They are taught to think about why authors write texts in a given manner. They are taught to recognize who is included as well as who is excluded and to discuss the reasoning behind such actions.

One final point I wish to make about my *reading well* model is this: while all components are essential and show themselves throughout the activities in this book, critical reading and critical literacy are front and center. Given the numerous advertisements, movies, and magazines that children encounter, teaching them how to take a critical stance is necessary to help dispel any potential myths evident in what they see and hear. Is it really true that eating sugar-coated cereal will make children as strong as the Superman displayed on the cereal box? Many adults know this is false advertising, but do children? Getting them to think about advertisements such as these and the motives behind them is what critical literacy is all about.

What Do I Mean by "Be Fit"?

Just as reading is defined in a variety of ways, so, too, is fitness. Some liken it to exercise. Take the President's Challenge, created in the 1950s by President Eisenhower, for example. Fitness is defined as exercise. Participants are assessed on five events to determine their level of fitness in five distinct areas: muscular strength/endurance, cardio-respiratory endurance, speed, agility, and flexibility (President's Council on Physical Fitness and Sports, 2004). When they pass all areas, they are fit.

Others propose a broader view of fitness. For instance, Graham, Hale, and Parker (2009) state, "In a broader sense, fitness is wellness—optimal health and well-being. In addition to physical fitness, wellness encompasses the dimensions of emotional, mental, spiritual, interpersonal/social, and environmental well-being" (p. 49). In other words, to focus on the total person, all these dimensions must be addressed giving individuals the opportunity to live enjoyable, fulfilling lives.

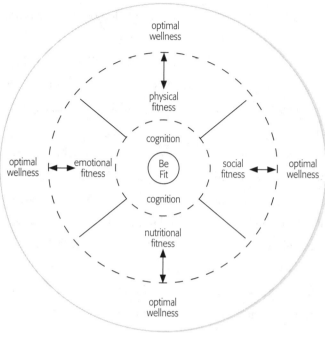

optimal
wellness

physical
fitness

cognition

optimal
wellness

emotional
fitness

Be
Fit

social
fitness

optimal
wellness

cognition

nutritional
fitness

optimal
wellness

▶ Figure 1.2 *Be Fit Model*

My definition reflects this more comprehensive view (see Figure 1.2). It includes five components that work together for optimal fitness and shows that cognition permeates all of them. To *be fit* means that individuals do the following:

1. ***Participate in some kind of physical activity.*** Physical activity is an important part of fitness. Making time for it every day better ensures that it becomes a routine. In fact, new U.S. Department of Health and Human Services guidelines (2008) suggest a minimum of 60 minutes daily for children. While this might appear excessive, it seems like a good time investment when we look at the benefits of physical activity (see Figure 1.3).

2. ***Get proper nutrition.*** Proper nutrition is a significant part of being fit. It enables children to have sustained energy throughout the day, to function better mentally, and to guard against health-related problems such as obesity and diabetes. In fact, the results of several studies have led researchers to a finding that appears to be common sense: good nutrition

Benefit	Result
Increase metabolic rate	Able to burn more body fat, becoming more lean
Lower blood pressure	Heart works more efficiently, making heart problems less likely
Improve heart and lung function	Able to perform daily activities with greater ease
Decrease the effects of stress	Less anxiety, increased concentration, increased academic performance
Weight loss and/or weight maintenance	Feel better about one's self and perform activities with greater ease; less chance of developing heart disease
Improve muscle tone, strength, flexibility, and coordination	Feel more confident in completing physical activities

▶ Figure 1.3 *Benefits of Physical Activity*

leads to better learning (Wahlstrom and Begalle, 1999). Think of it this way: garbage in, garbage out. Quality in, quality out.

3. Develop their intellects. One of the ways individuals continue to progress toward optimal health is to expand their intellects. As they continue to learn new information, learners strengthen their minds and increase their capacity to understand and solve problems. Self-esteem soars as students grasp new skills and take the necessary risks to apply them in meaningful contexts. Clearly, active learning keeps learners mentally sharp and supports their becoming interesting conversationalists.

4. Socialize. A large part of living a full life is being social in a variety of settings. Cultivating friendships and learning how to function in different groups, sometimes as leaders and other times as followers, are two outcomes of socializing. Socializing also helps children to discern the difference between appropriate and inappropriate behaviors relative to the situation at hand. In other words, they know how to read the social context and how to best adapt so that they can remain a part of the interaction rather than feel alienated from it. Halliday (1975) makes clear that socializing provides opportunities for children to learn

Function of Language		Use
Instrumental	("I want")	To satisfy needs or desires
Regulatory	("Do as I tell you!")	To control the behavior of others
Interactional	("Me and you")	To establish and keep relationships
Personal	("Here I come!")	To express one's personal feelings or thoughts
Heuristic	("Tell me why.")	To discover and find out why something happens
Imaginative	("Let's pretend.")	To create an imaginative world of one's own
Informative	("I have something to tell you.")	To provide information to others

▶ Figure 1.4 *Halliday's Functions of Language*

how to be flexible language users, those who use language in seven different ways for specific purposes (see Figure 1.4).

5. *Focus on emotional well-being.* Emotions—all humans have them, and part of being fit is recognizing how to embrace them. Feeling sad, happy, angry, and upset are natural states of being. Being able to express feelings and having others respond to us is a way of valuing ourselves. Keeping emotions bottled up within oneself only causes health-related problems such as depressed learning, memory loss, and decreased immunity (Hannaford, 1995).

Emotional well-being also entails self-esteem—how individuals feel about themselves relative to any given task. Being able to accomplish a task makes people feel better about themselves and yields higher self-esteem. In Kohn's words, ". . . there is very little about our personalities that does not flow from how we feel about ourselves" (1992, p. 99).

Self-esteem is both essential and dynamic. It rises and falls with given activities, as one's perceived abilities about being able to complete those activities (self-efficacy) rise and fall. There is potential for a spill-over effect from one content area to another. Having high self-esteem in fitness can spill over or create an "I can" belief in reading.

Two points about this *be fit* model are in order. First, as do the components that work together to enable *reading well*, so, too, do the fitness components team up for optimal wellness. *Physical activity*, for example, can lead individuals to *socialize* with others. *Proper nutrition* provides the amount of energy that is needed to complete a *physical activity*. To perform an *activity* properly, one has to know how to do it (cognition) and what is to be accomplished. And finally, *emotional well-being* comes into play when individuals have the confidence to participate in activities, paying close attention to how they feel about their performance and whether or not they want to participate again.

Second, just as learning to read well is a journey, so, too, is becoming fit. It is a lifestyle rather than a one-time event. Individuals need to constantly work at developing each part in order to realize their full potential. And as is shown in Figure 1.5, there is a reciprocal relationship between reading well and being fit, making optimal fitness more likely.

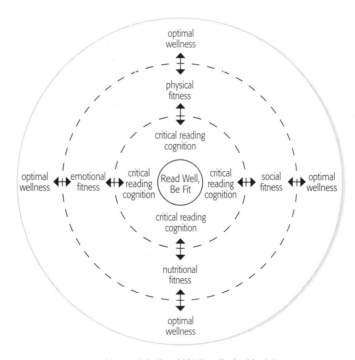

▶ Figure 1.5 Read Well to Be Fit Model

Why Integrate Reading and Fitness?

The idea of teaching with an integrated curriculum (teaching two or more content areas together) has been embraced by educators for years. The overriding goal is to help children better learn by showing them how different subjects are interrelated. (See Gavelek, Raphael, Biondo, and Wang, 2000, for a review of studies related to integrated instruction.) Through integration, children's understanding goes deeper and therefore has staying power. This is especially true with reading and fitness. In order to accomplish either or both, learners need to be active, purposeful, evaluative, thoughtful, strategic, persistent, and productive (Duke and Pearson, 2001). Indeed, there are thought processes that link reading and fitness (see Figure 1.6).

Under the banner of *interdisciplinary learning*, professional books such as *It's the Story That Counts* (Whitin and Wilde, 1992), *Significant Studies for Second Grade* (Ruzzo and Sacco, 2004), and *Science Workshop* (Saul, Reardon, Pearce, Dieckman, and Neutze, 2002) provide detailed explanations about how to integrate reading and the other language arts with specific content areas such as science, social studies, mathematics, and English. Yet very little has been written about how to integrate reading with fitness.

The current state of affairs regarding children's health (i.e., childhood obesity) is reason enough to extend the idea of integration to fitness. It's ironic that while we as a nation are beginning to recognize the problem, we are at the same time so obsessed with leaving "no child behind" that we may in fact be contributing to the epidemic. That is, in an effort to get higher test scores, recess is often cut and physical education programs are minimal, if they exist at all. Students who were once active on the school grounds are now inactive (Strauss, Rodzilsky, Burack, and Colin, 2001). And if you think that they get this activity after school, think again! *Inactive school children tend to be inactive after school, too* (Dale, Corbin, and Dale, 2000).

What's so bad about inactivity? It contributes to obesity (Welk and Blair, 2000; Waite-Stupiansky and Findlay, 2001). Waite-Stupiansky et al. also emphasize that children's

Literacy Lessons to Help Kids Get Fit & Healthy

Attributes	Reading	Fitness
Active	Readers read the text, bringing their own experiences to the text to construct meaning. They make predictions, make decisions such as what to read and reread and when to slow down or speed up.	One component of fitness is physical activity, which calls for active participation. However, participants also have to engage the intellectual aspect of fitness as they think about how to complete the exercise and what they might already know about the exercise or similar exercises to best complete it.
Purposeful	Readers have purposes in mind when they read a text. They then read with these purposes in mind. For example, they might choose to read for enjoyment or entertainment. At other times, they might read to discover specific details.	Fit individuals have definite purposes, which is what makes them select specific exercises, eat certain foods, and determine how to interact with different individuals.
Evaluative	Readers evaluate what they are reading, asking themselves if the text is meeting their initial purposes for reading it. They also evaluate the quality of the text and whether it is of value. They react to the text both emotionally and intellectually. Readers also evaluate their interaction with others in different instructional groupings as well as their ability to function as both leaders and followers in the group.	Fitness participants evaluate their performance when doing an exercise to determine their level of performance. They react to their levels of performance both emotionally and intellectually. At other times, they evaluate their diets to determine the appropriateness of food choices. At still other times, they evaluate their interaction with others and their ability to function as both leaders and followers.
Thoughtful	Readers think about the text selection before, during, and after reading. *Before reading* they think about what they might already know. *During reading*, they think about how the current text relates to what they already know. *After reading*, they think about what the text offered and their interpretations of it.	Fitness participants think about the physical activity they are engaged in. They also think about other areas of fitness, too. For example, they think about which foods are the best choices. They consider their feelings as they approach given tasks. They think about how they interact with others.
Strategic	Readers use specific strategies such as predicting, monitoring, and visualizing to ensure that they comprehend the text.	Fitness participants use strategies such as predicting, monitoring, and visualizing to ensure that they are completing a task correctly. They use monitoring, for example, when they chart their gains. They use visualizing as they see themselves performing an activity. They use predicting when they determine how they might perfect their performance the next time they complete the same activity.
Persistent	Readers keep reading a text even when it might be rather difficult, if they feel that the text is helping them to accomplish a set purpose.	Fitness participants stay with a task as long as they see that it is helping them to accomplish a specific purpose.
Productive	Readers are productive in more than one way. For instance, they bring their own experiences to the text at hand to construct or *produce* their understanding of it.	Researchers report over and over again that fit individuals are more productive at work and play. They also experience lower stress levels and have fewer bouts with illnesses, which enables them to be more productive.

▶ Figure 1.6 *Thought Processes That Link Reading and Fitness* blood pressure and cholesterol, two of the many ailments associated with childhood obesity, are escalating.

Integrating fitness and reading, then, is one way to combat this problem. The two can join forces to increase children's learning capacity and fight against obesity simultaneously. But there are still other sound reasons for integrating the two. Below are four.

Four Reasons for Integrating Reading and Fitness

1. *To motivate students.* Motivation is a powerful force in both reading and fitness. (Gambrell and Marniak, 1997; Guthrie and Wigfield, 2000). Sometimes an interest in fitness motivates reading. At other times, reading motivates fitness. Take the many readers who like to read the sports page of the newspaper. An interest in this aspect of fitness is the driving force behind the reading. Books about sports figures offer another example. And consider the many fitness-related magazines that interest children! Without a doubt, interests in issues surrounding fitness have the potential to motivate children to read.

On the other hand, reading about fitness can motivate readers to become more fit. For example, when reading selections that focus on how to run faster, readers are likely to try out some of the ideas mentioned in the reading (assuming that they are given time to do so). As a result of reading about nutritious meals and how to prepare them, readers are now in a good position to give them a try. What's more is that because the motivation is more intrinsic, learners are apt to complete the activity, be it reading or fitness, because they want to; they need no external reward.

What's problematic about using external rewards? First, while rewards such as candy or trinkets from a treasure box or principals performing stunts (e.g., shaving their heads, sitting on top of their schools for a full day) appear to motivate children to read at the onset, the results of several studies have led investigators to conclude that once the reward is no longer given, reading decreases. In fact, the reading of several children who initially read for their own enjoyment with no extrinsic reward can and often does *decrease when external rewards end*! (See Kohn, 1992 for a review of these studies).

Second, rewards can lead to poor health. Consider Pizza Hut's food-for-reading program, in which children get a free pizza for reading a given number of books. *The problem?* Commercial pizza is loaded with saturated fat, which raises cholesterol levels more than any other food in one's diet (AFFA, 2003). It is also high in calories. *The punishment?* Children associate reading with eating. No eating, no reading. It should come as no surprise that programs like this have created "a lot of fat kids who don't like to read" (Nicholls, 1999).

2. **To apply brain researchers' findings.** We have long known that physical activity is an excellent way for children to strengthen their bones and muscles. We also know that physical activity improves their circulation. Just as important, though, researchers are sharing much compelling evidence that when students engage in physical activity, their *reading test scores are likely to show greater gains* (Castelli, Hillman, Buck, and Erwin, 2007; Ericsson, 2003; Hines, 2001; Mears, 2003; Biernacki, 1993). Those who study the brain shed some light on why this might be so. Jensen (2000) and Jensen and Dabney (2000), for example, discovered that strenuous physical activity boosts brain activity, impacting reading the most. Other sample findings of the effects of physical activity on the brain are shown in Figure 1.7 (see Summerford, 2001 for additional information).

Researchers	*Brief Definition*	*Results*
Howard (2000) Jensen (2000) Jensen & Dabney (2000)	• Increases capillaries around the brain neurons, which increases blood and oxygen supply to the brain	Improves speed of recall
	• Releases endorphins	Increases alertness
Dienstbier (1989)	• Rapid adrenaline-nonadrenaline response and quick recovery	Ability to respond to mental challenges

▶ Figure 1.7 *Effects of Physical Activity on the Brain*

Clearly, children remember more when they are actively involved with both their bodies and minds (Ratey, 2008; Jensen, 2006; Stevens-Smith, 1999; Hannaford, 1995).

3. To differentiate instruction. More than 25 years ago, Gardner proposed his theory of multiple intelligences (Gardner, 1985). Three key ideas of his theory are that a) there are several intelligences, b) individuals possess all of them to some degree or another and some are more developed than others, and c) identifying and nurturing these intelligences are ways to help all individuals maximize their potential. They are then better equipped to solve problems. One of these intelligences is *bodily kinesthetic*. Those who are strong in this intelligence have a tendency to be active in several ways (e.g., taking things apart and reassembling them; moving, twitching, or fidgeting when seated; participating in sports) (Armstrong, 1994).

This knowledge reflects the need to differentiate instruction in an effort to reach and teach as many children as possible. It also suggests a relatively easy way to integrate fitness and reading. For instance, children can show their understanding of reading content through some sort of physical activity. Teachers can invite students to show understanding of a text by acting out a scene from something they have read.

Moreover, researchers investigating boys and literacy also hint at the need to differentiate. They note that boys need movement and different kinds of texts (e.g., action-oriented) to get and keep engaged with reading (Tyre, 2008). Once again, variety beckons in order to reach and teach the masses.

4. To save time. With so much subject matter to teach, each with its own set of standards, it is no wonder that some content areas get short-changed. Integration is one of the ways to take another look at this short-changing. Just as with other subject areas (e.g., social studies and reading), so, too, can fitness be integrated with other content areas (Buell and Whittaker, 2001; Cone and Cone, 2001; Marlett and Gordon, 2004; Siegel, 2000). Fitness provides a valuable circuit for helping children excel at reading (Baldwin, 1982; Bennet and Hanneleen, 2003; Dwyer, Sallis, Blizzard, Lazarus, and Dean, 2001; Lasala, 1993).

How Can Reading and Fitness Be Integrated?

As with reading and physical fitness definitions, there are several explanations about how to design an integrated curriculum (e.g., Barnes, 2007; Fogarty, 1991). Reviewing these models led me to conclude that the shared model (Fogarty, 1991) is most useful for the activities I propose in this text. Here's why:

A shared model entails bringing two content areas together through overlapping concepts. Fogarty (1991) says it best: "The shared model views the curriculum through binoculars, bringing two distinct disciplines together into a single focused image." As it pertains to this book, then, reading and fitness are the two content areas. Active learning is an example of an overlapping concept. That is, we teach students how to be active readers and also point out how they use similar processes when engaged in fitness. Or we teach an aspect of physical fitness such as evaluating how well they performed an activity, and point out how they evaluate when they read.

Although two teachers can use the shared model when planning together, one teacher can go it alone, fitting the integrated lessons delineated in this book into existing classroom routines (e.g., guided reading). For those of you fortunate enough to work with willing, knowledgeable colleagues, I have included Tips for Collaborating With Other Specialists throughout the book.

I also endorse using critical literacy as a meaningful way to achieve this integration. For example, making children aware of food labels and teaching them how to read and analyze them helps children understand what it is they are purchasing and how it contributes (or not) to their daily diet. Are they getting what they think they are getting?

Figure 1.8 provides an overview of the fitness categories, reading comprehension skills, physical fitness skills, and the specific lesson that brings unity. Chapters 2–5 each showcase a different physical fitness category and offer explanations of the various lessons.

		PHYSICAL FITNESS					NUTRITION FITNESS				
	Areas of Fitness	Catch the Beat (Cardio, Endurance)	Tough It Out! (Muscle Strength and Endurance)	Bone Strength! (Bone Strengthening)	What Are You Made Of? (Body Composition)	Bend a Little! (Flexibility)	Shape Up! (MyPyramid for Kids)	Go, Slow, or Whoa? (Different Foods)	What's In This? (Reading Food Labels)	Portion or Serving? (Serving Sizes)	What's the Trick? (Advertising Tricks)
Background	Brainstorming										
	Anticipation Guide		X								
	Prediction Guide	X									
	Problem Perspective									X	
Vocabulary	Concept Circle						X				
	Word Map Four Square				X						
	Knowledge Rating					X		X			
	List, Group, Label										
	Semantic Feature Analysis										
Comprehension/Discussion	Discussion Web										
	Double-Entry Journal										
	Guided Reading Procedure										
	Idea Circle										
	Intra-Act										
	Questioning the Author										
	Selective Reading Guide										
Text Structure	External Text Structure								X		
	Internal Text Structure										
	Network Tree			X							
	Text Annotations										
Critical Literacy	Alternate Perspectives										
	Evaluating Images										X
	Detecting Bias/Propaganda Techniques										
	Posing Problems									X	
	Juxtaposing										
	Taking Action	X	X	X	X	X	X	X	X	X	X

► Figure 1.8 *Overview Chart*

	SOCIAL FITNESS					EMOTIONAL FITNESS				
Acts of Kindness	True Friends	Appreciating and Including Others	Manners, Please!	Don't Be Bullied!	Here's Looking at You! (Positive Self-image)	How Do You Feel? (Emotions)	You Can Do It! (Self-efficacy)	Set and Meet a Goal (Goal Setting)	Solve Your Problem! (Making Decisions)	
	X									
		X								
								X		
						X				
X										
									X	
			X							
		X								
							X			
				X						
			X						X	
		X		X						
									X	
				X		X				
X	X	X	X	X	X	X	X	X	X	

CHAPTER 2

Integrating
PHYSICAL FITNESS
AND LITERACY

The importance of physical fitness is in the media spotlight these days, and for good reason. Children simply are not moving enough and they are suffering poor health as a result. Many of today's children are suffering with health ailments such as heart disease, diabetes, and sleep apnea, three conditions that in the past were associated with adults. In fact, some health educators predict that unless something drastic happens to change children's fitness conditions, theirs will be the first generation in history to die at a younger age than their parents.

In addition to the problems associated with lack of physical activity are the more enlightening findings of researchers investigating the impact of physical activity on academic achievement (see Chapter 1). In short, students who are physically active tend to perform better in mathematics and reading, especially reading comprehension (Hillman et al., 2009).

That physical fitness is important, then, is not in question. What *is* often in question relates to the terms *physical fitness* and *physical activity*. Just what is physical fitness? According to the Centers for Disease Control (1996), there are five main components of physical fitness (see Figure 2.1). Individually and collectively, all of these components are

Component	Brief Definition
Cardiorespiratory endurance	Ability of the body to supply fuel during sustained physical activity
Muscle strength	Ability of the muscle to exert force during an activity
Muscle endurance	Ability of the muscle to continue to perform without fatigue
Body composition	Relative amount of muscle, fat, bone, and other vital parts of the body
Flexibility	Range of motion around a joint

▶ Figure 2.1 *Components of Physical Fitness*

ways to engage in *physical activity* (i.e., "bodily movement that enhances health" US Dept of Health and Human Services, 2008, p. 5).

Helping children develop an understanding of these areas with an emphasis on being *physically active* is the purpose of this chapter. The overall goal is to help children understand how to use literacy as one tool to better understand the importance of being physically active. Figure 2.2 is an overview of the physical fitness activities and content literacy teaching strategies this chapter showcases.

	Catch the Beat (Cardio, Endurance)	Tough It Out (Muscular Str & End)	Bone Strength! (Bone Strengthening)	What Are You Made Of? (Body Composition)	Bend a Little! (Flexibility)
Anticipation Guide		X			
Prediction Guide	X				
Word Map Four Square				X	
Knowledge Rating					X
Network Tree			X		
Taking Action	X	X	X	X	X

▶ Figure 2.2 *Physical Fitness Lessons/Content Literacy Teaching Strategies*

Catch the Beat

Description

Physical Fitness: As noted in the 2008 Physical Activity Guidelines for Americans (HHS, 2008), there are many types of physical activity. Aerobic activity (cardiovascular endurance) is one. Examples of aerobic activity include running, hopping, skipping, jumping rope, and bicycling. This type of physical activity causes the heart to beat faster than when being inactive because it moves blood through the heart at a faster rate, causing the heart to work harder. One benefit of aerobic activity is that it strengthens the heart. To get the most out of it, children should be engaged with this type of activity for 60 or more minutes daily (HHS, 2008, p. 16).

Reading: Encouraging readers to activate their thinking about the content to be read is one way to build interest and better ensure comprehension. Using some kind of prediction strategy such as posing a question and providing students time to discuss it is one way to accomplish this. Students are able to think about what they might already know about the topic at hand as well as what they might want to know.

FitLit Suggestions

Title	Author	Publisher/Year	Suggested Grade Levels
The Busy Body Book: A Kid's Guide to Fitness	Lizzy Rockwell	Crown/2004	K–2
Exercise and Play	Cath Senker	PowerKids Press/2008	K–2
Get Up and Go!	Nancy Carlson	Viking/2006	K–2
Why Should I Get Off the Couch? and Other Questions About Health and Exercise	Louise Spilsbury	Heinemann/2003	1–4

Tying physical fitness and reading together, Catch the Beat enables students to use a literacy skill (making predictions) to learn about their pulse rate and discover how physical activity increases it. They also learn why periodically increasing their heart rate is beneficial to their overall health and how to document their own physical activity.

Teaching Procedures

1. Give students a sticky note and ask them to write their names on it.

2. Show students how to take their pulse (see Figure 2.3). Explain that pulse rate is how many times their heart beats in one minute. It is felt as blood is pushed through an artery located in their wrists. Once students have their rate, have them write it on their sticky notes.

3. Ask them what they think might happen to their pulse rate if they start to move. Do they think it will stay the same? Increase? Decrease?

4. Have students place their sticky notes in the column that corresponds to their answer and to provide reasons for their choices.

5. Give each student a physical activity to complete, such as marching in place for one minute.

6. Have them take their pulses and write down the number.

7. Have them check their predictions. Were they correct? Did their number stay the same? Increase? Decrease?

8. Provide time for students to discuss why they think their heart rate went up.

9. Point out that completing physical activities to increase heart rate strengthens the heart. Emphasize that they can take action for developing healthy hearts by being physically active. Brainstorm the kind of activities they can do in and out of school and write their suggestions on a chart large enough for all to see.

10. Provide each with a "taking action" form and explain how to use it.

Classroom Voices

Keith wants his second graders to better understand how heart rate relates to their overall health. He also wants them to see that making predictions is a skill that can be used in many content areas. He decides to do a whole-group lesson and calls the students to the meeting area. Once all are settled, he comments, "You have been learning a lot about what good readers do when they read. You know that one thing they do is make predictions before and during reading. But did you know that you can also make predictions when learning about other subjects, such as fitness? That's exactly what I am going to show you today. We're going to use making predictions to learn something about your heart rates."

He continues by asking, "What do you think I mean by heart rate? Let's make some predictions." As students provide their comments, Keith writes them on the SMART Board so that all can see. He then comments, "Let's see if any of your predictions are accurate." Keith then shows students how to take their pulse rates by first demonstrating how to do so himself. He then asks for a volunteer so that he can demonstrate with a student. Finally, he has students take their own heart rate and write the number on their sticky notes.

"Because you were sitting still, or resting, when you took your heart rate, the number you just wrote on your sticky note is called a resting heart rate," Keith comments. "What

---

How to Measure Your Pulse Rate

1. Hold out your left hand with your palm facing up.
2. Place your right fingertips on your left wrist.
3. Press firmly to feel the thump of your pulse.
4. Count the beats for 60 seconds.
5. Write the number of total beats you count during the 60 seconds.
6. This is your resting heart rate.

Normal resting heart rate for children is 80–90 beats per minute.

* Adapted from *Heartaware* (p. 5). Heart Center of the Rockies, Fort Collins, CO.

Figure 2.3 *How to Measure Your Pulse Rate*

Literacy Lessons to Help Kids Get Fit & Healthy

do you think might happen to it if I have you do some marching in place? Let's make some predictions. If you think it is going to increase, put your sticky note in the column on the board that says 'Increase.' If you think it is going to decrease, put it in that column. And if you think that it is going to stay the same, put it in the 'Stay the same' column." Keith gives students time to place their sticky notes in the appropriate column. He then says, "Ok, now I want you to stand up and when I say to begin, march in place until I say that time is up. Ready? Begin."

After one minute, Keith stops students and instructs them to take their heart rates again. He then has them write their number on their sticky notes. "So what happened? Were your predictions accurate?" After some students volunteer their responses, Keith notes, "You discovered that when you move, your heart rate goes up. Do you know why?"

"I think it's because the heart is working harder," says Heidi. "And you are exactly right," Keith assures. He continues, "When you move, you make your heart work harder. It has to push blood in and out more quickly than when you are sitting still. Working harder makes your heart get stronger, just as using your body to move and do physical tasks makes your body stronger. So if you want to have a strong heart, you have to move. You have to be physically active. Let's think of some ways that you can be physically active. I'll write them on this chart."

Keith closes the lesson by stating, "Being active is very important in order to be healthy. One way you can make sure you are being active and taking control of your health is to keep a list of the activities you do. You can use this chart to do just that." He then distributes the chart (see Figure 2.4) and shows students how to complete it.

Extensions

1. Consider having children in Grades 3–4 read the article titled "Why Exercise Is Cool," which can be accessed at *www.kidshealth.org*, to both verify and extend the information about the benefits of exercise. Individual students can read the whole article or different groups of students can read the different sections of it and report to the rest of the class.

My Physical Activity Log	
Name _____ Week _____	
Day	**Activities I Performed**

Figure 2.4 *Taking Action: My Physical Activities*

2. Invite students to think and draw a picture of a physical activity they can do instead of sitting. Then provide each with the sentence frame, "Instead of sitting, I can _____." Have students write the sentence and complete it with the word that names their activity so that their sentence tells about their picture. Once all have finished, call the class together and provide time for volunteers to read and show their pages. Once sharing is complete, gather all pages and assemble them into a class book titled "How We Move" and place it in the classroom library for all to read.

3. Another way for students in the upper elementary grades to calculate heart rate is to count the number of beats for ten seconds and multiply by six to get the total. Using this technique would provide a meaningful way for older students to apply what they know about multiplication.

Web Sites

www.cdc.gov/healthyyouth/physicalactivity/brochures/index.htm provides access to brief yet informative brochures designed to give parents and educators additional information about physical activity and some practical tips.

www.gameskidsplay.net provides a wealth of games that enhance physical activities.

www.americanheart.org provides several lessons about the heart and the effects of physical exercise.

Tips for Professional Collaboration

School Nurse: Work in collaboration with the school nurse to schedule a time to provide students with additional information about the heart.

Tough It Out

Description

Physical Fitness: As important as cardio-respiratory activities are, they are not enough. Children also need to do activities that will strengthen their muscles. While it is true that many everyday activities—such as walking up steps, carrying a book bag to school, and throwing a ball to the family dog—all help to strengthen muscles, muscle-strengthening activities go a step further. As noted in the 2008 Physical Activity Guidelines for Americans (HHS, 2008), muscle-strengthening activities make one's muscles do more work than usual. They overload the muscles, making them stronger. And, when these activities are done over a period of time, they enable individuals to develop muscular endurance, the ability to repeat the activity without much fatigue. A benefit of this type of activity is that it enables children to perform daily activities with greater ease. Physical appearance is another benefit. That is, the activities help to develop both muscle shape and tone (Hastie and Martin, 2006).

Use of playground equipment such as monkey bars and playground games such as tug of war build muscular strength and endurance. Working with stretch bands is another way to help children develop muscular strength and endurance. Regardless of the activity, children need to complete muscle-strengthening and endurance activities at least three times a week as a part of their 60-minute physical activity daily allotment (HHS, p. 16).

Reading: There are many ways to activate students' thinking about the content they are to read that are likely to increase their comprehension of the material. An "anticipation guide" is one such activity. It is a series of statements that students think about and respond to before reading the related text. It encourages them to raise expectations about the meaning of the text before they read it. Students often revisit the guide after reading and discuss their findings.

Using both physical fitness and reading, Tough It Out enables students to learn about their muscles by first using their own background to make some decisions about what they think an author will share with them. They then use discussion to further refine their understandings. Finally, students discuss the implications of physical activity and how they might take action to ensure that they engage with muscular strength and endurance activities.

FitLit Suggestions

Title	Author	Publisher/Year	Suggested Grade Levels
Fitness for Fun	Dana Meadren Rau	Capstone Press/2009	K–2
Jungle Gym	Stephen Krensky	Simon & Schuster Inc./2008	K–1
Playground Day!	Jennifer Merz	Houghton Mifflin Company/2007	K–1
Take It to the Hoop, Magic Johnson	Quincy Troupe	Hyperion Books for Children/2000	1–3
Why Must I Exercise?	Jackie Goff	Cherry Tree Books/2005	3–5

Literacy Lessons to Help Kids Get Fit & Healthy

Teaching Procedures

1. Create an "anticipation guide" for the text you will be using. Here's how:

- Read through the text and determine what you want to call students' attention to.

- Write a statement for each idea.

- After each statement, provide a column for students to indicate whether they agree or disagree with the statement.

2. Decide how you want to use the anticipation guide. You might want to display one copy on the overhead projector or create one copy on a chart large enough for all to see.

3. Gather the children in the meeting area. Engage children with several different paired movements, such as clenching their fingers and opening them, bending and lengthening their arms, and standing and squatting.

4. Provide time for children to talk about what enabled them to make these movements, and list their comments on a chart large enough for all to see.

5. Tell students that they will be listening to a text about muscles, but that before they do, they need to complete the anticipation guide.

6. Display the guide, explain how to use it, and provide time for students to complete it.

7. Read the text to the children.

8. After reading, have students take another look at the anticipation guide and reflect on their initial responses. Provide time for students to discuss the statements and whether or not they would change any statements based on their reading.

9. Based on their reading, have children discuss how they can take action to make sure that they are doing physical activities that will give them both muscular strength and endurance.

Classroom Voices

To enhance her third-grade students' comprehension abilities and their understanding of the importance of muscle strength and endurance for physical activity, Brenda selects *Muscles* (Simon, 1998) as a read-aloud. After students are seated in the whole-group meeting area, she states, "Let's do some movements. I'll show you how and you follow my lead. Ready? Clench your fingers and open them. Now bend your arm and straighten it. OK. Stand up and squat down, as if you are going to sit on a chair. All right. That's enough! Go ahead and sit down." Brenda continues by asking students to think about what enabled them to make the various movements and writes their comments on the board. She says, "I think you have some excellent ideas. In fact, I think they are a lot like what the author includes in the book I am going to read to you today." She holds up a copy of the book *Muscles* for all to see. "But before I read and you listen, let's do one more thing. Let's take a look at this guide (see Figure 2.5). Let's read each item and decide if we agree or disagree with it." In turn, Brenda reads each statement and takes a count of students who agree or disagree with it. She writes that number in the correct column on the guide. Once the guide is completed, Brenda reads as students listen.

Anticipation Guide for Muscles		
Directions: Take a look at each statement. Do you agree or disagree?		
Statement	**Agree**	**Disagree**
1. You can control all of your muscles.		
2. There are at least three kinds of muscles.		
3. Exercise strengthens your muscles.		
4. If you do not exercise, your muscles will shrink and you will get tired very easily.		
5. Muscles enable you to move.		

▶ Figure 2.5 *Anticipation Guide for Muscles*

Taking Action for Muscle Strength and Endurance

My Name _____   Date _____

Here's what I will do to make sure I develop muscle strength and endurance:

In school: _____

Out of school: _____

▶ Figure 2.6 *Taking Action for Muscle Strength and Endurance*

Brenda then asks students to take another look at the anticipation guide. "Now that you have listened to the book, let's revisit each of these statements to see if we still think like we did before reading and listening." She provides time for students to discuss each statement. She also refers them back to their initial chart of reasons they thought they were able to make movements, to see if there is anything that connects with the text.

Brenda then takes the students a step further by commenting, "One of the best ways to strengthen muscles is to be physically active. But what kinds of activities do you think you need to do? Let's list some here." Brenda concludes the lesson stating, "Being physically active is important for several reasons. The reason you learned about today is that being active helps your muscles to get stronger. And stronger muscles help you to participate in activities for longer periods of time. How are you going to use what you know to take some action? Write your goal on your taking action card." (See Figure 2.6.)

Extensions

1. Invite students to research a specific activity they like to perform. They can research to determine different ways to perform the activity and the muscles it helps to develop. Students can then report their findings, either to a small group or the whole class.

Consider making a class compilation of these different activities. Students can consult the "class directory" when looking for alternate activities.

2. To increase students' understanding, have them select a text and create an anticipation guide for it. They can then pair up. Partners can take turns sharing their guides, listening to the text, and discussing the guide after the text has been read.

Web Sites

www.kidshealth.org provides additional information about muscles, including a brief animated cartoon, diagrams, and a muscle quiz.

www.smartspot.com offers much information to help professionals teach children about different kinds of physical activity (as well as how to balance food intake with the type of physical activity to be performed).

Tips for Professional Collaboration

Physical Educator: Ask the physical education instructor to show children the My Pyramid for Kids chart (see Appendix B) and point out the kinds of activities students will be completing during the class session. Make clear those activities that are helping children to develop both muscular strength and endurance.

Bone Strength!

Description

Physical Fitness: Bone-strengthening is a third type of physical activity. Like the other two types of physical activity (aerobic and muscle-strengthening), bone-strengthening should be a part of the 60-minute daily physical activity at least three days of the week (HHS, 2008,

p. 16). The necessity of this type of activity seems obvious. Like a house, strong bones make for a firm foundation that can withstand a lot of force. Any kind of activity that produces force or stress on the bones is considered to be bone-strengthening. Jumping rope, basketball, and hopscotch are just a few examples.

Reading: All texts are constructed using some type of structure. A tremendous amount of research has led many different researchers to conclude that children need to be taught these structures as a way of increasing their understanding of text. Using graphic organizers is one way to make a visual representation of these different structures. The network tree is one such display. It enables teachers to show students the relationships among the larger ideas and supporting ideas within a text.

Linking physical fitness and reading, Bone Strength! enables students to use a text structure to better understand how their bones relate to one another. Exploring the many bones of the body leads to ways that students can use physical activity to make them stronger.

FitLit Suggestions

Title	Author	Publisher/Year	Suggested Grade Levels
Action Alphabet	Shelly Rotner	Atheneum Books for Young Readers/1996	K–1
Bones: Our Skeletal System	Seymour Simon	Morrow/1998	3–5
Hoops	Robert Burleigh	Harcourt Brace & Company/1997	2–5
Rimshots: Basketball Pix, Rolls, and Rhythms	Charles R. Smith	Dutton Children's Books/1999	3–5
Sports	Wendy Barish	Scholastic/1994	K–2

Teaching Procedures

1. Select a text such as *You Can't See Your Bones With Binoculars* (Ziefert, 2003) that will enable students to learn about their bones.

2. Create a network tree for the text you will be using. Here's how (based on Vacca and Vacca, 2008):

- Look through the book (or chapter) to determine the most important vocabulary. Make a list of those words.

- Arrange the list of words. Choose the word that provides the overarching, inclusive idea of all selected words.

- Classify the other words accordingly underneath the larger concept.

- Make a visual display of all words that you will share with students. You may also choose to show the visual display without the words and add the words as the lesson progresses.

3. Provide students with an overview of the text by showing the blank network tree. It is intended to show the relationship of the main and supporting concepts. A complete network tree about the skeleton might look like this:

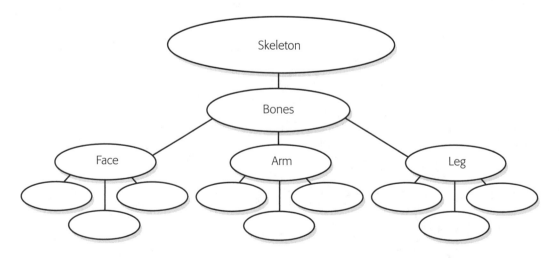

4. As you read through the text, add words to the network tree.

5. Once reading is finished, review all terms with students.

6. Discuss with students how knowing about their bones relates to their overall physical fitness.

7. Have students reflect on how they can take action to make sure that they are developing strong bones.

Classroom Voices

Lois is a first-grade teacher who believes that students read to learn and learn to read from the start. Not surprisingly, then, she has been teaching students about how authors of nonfiction texts craft their ideas. But she also sees text structure as a perfect way for her students to better understand not only text structure, but also their bone structure. She selects *You Can't See Your Bones With Binoculars* (Ziefert, 2003) to help her accomplish her goals. What's more, because of the way the book is written, she can invite students to do some of the reading. They can read the simpler text and she will read the more complex text that extends and elaborates the key ideas. Additionally, she has made word cards that she will highlight and add to the network tree during the reading.

Lois opens the lesson commenting, "All year long you have been learning that different authors use different ways to tell their ideas. This author is no different, and you're going to discover the many different words she uses to tell you more about your bones. I am going to call your attention to some of the most important words by hanging them on our life-size skeleton. But let's do some actions first." Lois then takes the students through the book for enjoyment, having them touch the bone that is highlighted on a given page. Once all have experienced the book, Lois states, "Now that you know a little bit about how your bones are connected, let's get some additional information. We'll reread the book. You chime in when you see the colored strip on the top of the page. Then I'll read the rest of the information the author provides." Lois takes the students through the book a second time and highlights the words she thinks students should remember by affixing them to the skeleton. Once the reading is finished, Lois says, "Look at our skeleton! Just like the way the author wrote the book, our bodies also have a specific structure, and this skeleton proves it! We even have names for the different bones. Let's review them." She then points to each label and students read in unison.

"There's just one other thing we need to think about before we end our lesson today. Now that you know more about your bones, how do you think you can make them strong so that they can hold up your body? Share your ideas with your neighbor and I'll then have a few of you give us your ideas." After giving students time to discuss their ideas, she asks for volunteers to share their idea with the larger group. Jennifer states, "I think that you need to eat good food to get healthy bones." Paul adds, "But I think you also have to do things like running." Lois responds, "Actually, you are both correct. Eating healthy foods and being physically active are both important for healthy bones." She concludes the lesson by having students think about what they might be able to do to make sure that they eat right and get some physical activity; she provides them with time to fill out their Taking Action card.

Taking Action for Bone Strength
My Name _____ Date _____
Here's what I will do to make sure I develop bone strength:
In school: _____
Out of school: _____

▶ Figure 2.7 *Taking Action for Bone Strength*

Extensions

1. Hastie and Martin (2006) suggest playing *Bone Hokey Pokey* as a way to reinforce students' understanding of the various bones. Play a musical rendition of "The Hokey Pokey" and invite students to put in various bones when called out.

2. Encourage students to seek out more information about various bones and specific physical activities individuals can do to ensure that their bones are strengthened. Students can choose the bone they want to research or they can draw one from a bag that contains labels for many different bones.

3. Invite students to read the suggested titles of their choosing.

Web Sites

www.cdc.gov/powerfulbones presents guidelines to help girls develop strong bones.

www.nichd.nih.gov/milk explains to children the importance of calcium as it relates to building strong bones.

www.hhs.gov/kids provides a listing of many different Web sites from which children can choose to explore many different fitness topics.

Tips for Professional Collaboration

School Nurse: Invite the school nurse to bring in some sample bones or a life-size skeleton and provide additional information about bones.

What Are You Made Of?

Description

Physical Fitness: While not necessarily a specific type of physical activity, body composition is the result of it. That is, as students perform different aerobic, muscle-strengthening, and bone-strengthening activities, they add to the muscle, fat, and bone that make up their total body composition. While paying attention to total weight is important, even more important is paying attention to how that weight breaks down. In other words, what we want is more weight to come from lean mass (i.e., muscle, bone, tendons, and ligaments) than from fat. One of the reasons to pay attention to body composition, then, is to manage a healthy weight.

Reading: Students need to understand that every content area, including physical fitness, has its own specialized vocabulary. They also need to learn how to associate and categorize words in order to develop a deeper understanding of the content they are learning. This is exactly what the Four-Square Word Map accomplishes. Through it, students learn meanings for words. They also apply their understanding by providing their own personal connection to the word.

FitLit Suggestions

Title	Author	Publisher/Year	Suggested Grade Levels
From Head to Toe	Barbara Seuling	Holiday House/2002	3–5
Human Body	Linda Calabresi	Simon & Schuster Inc./2007	3–5
The Human Body	Seymour Simon	HarperCollins Children's Books/2008	3–5
The Magic School Bus Inside the Human Body	Joanna Cole	Scholastic/1990	1–4
Wave Goodbye	Rob Reid	Lee and Low/1996	K–1

Dovetailing physical fitness and reading, What Are You Made Of? provides students with an opportunity to learn about body composition and the terms associated with the various parts.

Teaching Procedures

1. Divide a piece of paper into four parts.

2. Label each square with the following labels: *word, personal connection, text definition,* and *example.*

3. Have students fill in the distinguishing features for a given word, using the form shown in Figure 2.8.

Word	Personal Connection
Text Definition	Example

▶ Figure 2.8 *Four-Square Word Map*

Classroom Voices

To further help his fifth-grade students understand terms associated with body composition, Joe decides to use the four-square word map. He divides the students into four groups and gives each group a different word associated with body composition: *muscle, fat, bone, tendon, ligament.* He has also preselected the text *Human Anatomy* (Williams, 2008) and plans to give one page to each group. Each two-page spread includes a jigsaw puzzle and an information page related to a given aspect of human anatomy (e.g., muscular system). Joe will have each group complete the puzzle and read the additional information. He will also have them complete the four-square word map using the word assigned to their group. Finally, Joe will have each group report out to the others to share what they have learned about their word.

Extensions

1. To help students learn more interesting facts about the human body, consider using *100 Things You Should Know About Your Body* (Parker, 2003). Print each numeral, 1–100, on an index card and put the index cards into a paper bag. Have students draw a number from the bag, locate the corresponding fact in the book, practice reading it, and then read it to interested others.

2. Using the book *The Blood-Hungry Spleen and Other Poems About Our Parts* (Wolf, 2003), provide students time to select a poem about a given body part and prepare to read it during a poetry reading.

Web Sites

www.educationworld.com presents several physical fitness lesson plans. It also provides descriptions of exercises.

www.keepkidshealthy.com provides a wealth of information regarding fitness. Included are ideas for developing a physical fitness routine, from warm-up to cool-down!

Tips for Professional Collaboration

School Counselor: As a way of helping students better understand body image and how they feel about their looks, ask the school counselor to share insights with children.

Bend a Little!

Description

Physical Fitness: As with the other components of physical fitness, flexibility (i.e., the range of motion around a joint) is an important ingredient. And what better way to become flexible than by some form of stretching? It helps keep the muscles, ligaments, and tendons pliable and loose. According to Hastie and Martin (2006, p. 421), "Flexibility is necessary for improving and maintaining postural alignment, for executing movements efficiently and gracefully, and for facilitating and developing motor skills." The more flexible one is, the

FitLit Suggestions

Title	Author	Publisher/Year	Suggested Grade Levels
Because	Mikhail Baryshnikov	Atheneum/2007	2–3
From Head to Toe	Eric Carle	HarperCollins/1997	1
The Happiest Tree: A Yoga Story	Uma Krishnaswami	Lee and Low/2005	1–3
I Love Yoga	Mary Kaye Chryssicas	DK Publishing, Inc./2005	K–2
Twist: Yoga Poems	Janet Wong	McElderry/2007	2–5

more one can bend and reach. Hastie and Marin also note that flexibility is best achieved with slow and sustained stretching. Both slow and sustained are what yoga exercises are all about!

Reading: A "knowledge rating" (Blachowicz and Fisher, 2006) is a prereading vocabulary activity that helps children become aware of words related to the lesson they will experience. It also provides an opportunity for students to activate any prior knowledge they might have related to the words. Using the knowledge rating before and after reading, also helps children see that an in-depth understanding of words occurs over time.

Connecting physical fitness and reading, Bend a Little! enables students to become more flexible. They use vocabulary to learn about stretching in general and yoga in particular.

Teaching Procedures

1. Select key words that relate to the lesson.

2. Ask students to evaluate their understanding of the words by reading each term and checking the appropriate column: A Lot, Have Heard It, or No Idea (see Figure 2-9).

3. Provide students with time to discuss the words and what they think the lesson will be about.

4. Revisit the terms once the lesson is completed. Discuss whether or not they feel they have changed their minds about the words: Can they now define those they were not able to define at the start of the lesson?

Classroom Voices

As a way to help her fourth-grade students become more flexible, Karen has decided to teach them some yoga exercises. She has selected several cards from *Yoga Pretzels* (Guber and Kalish, 2005). After modeling one of the exercises, she will distribute the remaining cards to different groups of students, have them rehearse how to perform the exercise, and finally, teach others in the class. She decides to create some interest in the lesson by

Yoga Knowledge Rating			
Your Name _____ How much do you know about these words?			
Word:	**A Lot**	**Have Heard It**	**No Idea**
Dragon stretch			
Cat stretch			
Twisting dragon			
Pretzel			
Lying twist			
Cobra back bend			
Bridge back bend			

▶ Figure 2.9 *Yoga Knowledge Rating*

Literacy Lessons to Help Kids Get Fit & Healthy

using a knowledge rating (see Figure 2.9). She distributes the knowledge rating to the class and provides time for each to complete it independently. When the class is finished, she asks, "Now that you have taken a look at the words we are going to be using in this lesson, do you have any idea about what we might be learning?" Carl responds, "Well, I think it might have something to do with stretching because a couple of the terms have the word *stretch*." Others agree and Karen concedes. She then tells students that they will be learning how to do some yoga exercises. As with other lessons, Karen wants to make sure that students know why they are doing what they are doing. She asks, "Why do you think it would be important for you to do yoga? Think for a minute. Then turn and share with your neighbor." After providing this discussion time, Karen asks for volunteers to share their ideas. "Well, I think it is important because stretching will help us reach and bend," says Jeff. Connie then comments, "I agree. I think it will help us to be flexible and if we are flexible, we will probably not get injured."

Karen comments, "I agree with you and so do other experts who teach people about physical fitness. Let's go ahead and try one. I'll show you how to do the dragon stretch." She shows students the card that shows the picture of the movement on the front side and the directions for completing it on the reverse. After taking them through the exercise, she comments, "You did an excellent job of completing the dragon stretch. Now it is your turn to teach others some additional exercises." She instructs children to assemble into their buddy groups. Once in their groups, she continues, "I am going to give each group a card. What you need to do is prepare the exercise for the rest of us. Keep practicing until I call time. I'll be around to help."

The lesson proceeds with Karen giving students time to prepare and teach their exercises to others. Once the class is finished, she directs students back to the knowledge rating and has them take another look at the terms, commenting, "Now that you have experienced the different yoga exercises, take another look at your knowledge rating sheet. Let's talk about the terms." After students talk about the terms, Karen has students rerate their understanding of them by individually marking the columns using another color of pen.

Taking Action: Bend a Little							

Your Name _____

Exercise:	Sunday	Monday	Tuesday	Wednesday	Thursday	Friday	Saturday
Dragon stretch							
Cat stretch							
Twisting dragon							
Pretzel							
Lying twist							
Cobra back bend							
Bridge back bend							

▶ Figure 2.10 *Taking Action for Bend a Little*

Karen closes the lesson stating, "Today you learned some words about yoga and you also learned more about different ways to stretch so that you can remain flexible. You can now use these at home as one way to be physically active. Here's a form you can use to keep track of the different exercises." She distributes the Taking Action Form shown in Figure 2.10.

Extensions

1. Consider having students locate additional stretching exercises that they can teach to others in the class.

2. When using additional cards from *Yoga Pretzels*, have students first teach the exercise and see if the class can guess the name of the exercise, based on the movements. Once confirmed, add the title of the exercise to an ongoing list posted in the classroom. One way to extend students' understanding of how the words connect would be to provide them with time to make a visual display of the words.

Web Sites

www.kidsrunning.com provides information about appropriate ways for children to stretch before they do a big run.

www.paratec.com provides a chart of 20 stretches for children. Children fill out the opening form, which includes the version they want to have e-mailed to them.

Tips for Professional Collaboration

Media Specialist: There is debate about the value of stretching. Ask the media specialist to have children use the Internet to research the pros and cons about stretching and to discover what the arguments are. A good place to begin is with the article "Does Stretching Help?" available at *www.sciencenewsforkids.org*

CHAPTER 3

Integrating
NUTRITION FITNESS AND LITERACY

Hardly a day goes by without news of important childhood health issues. Childhood obesity, in particular, is in the media spotlight, often with startling statistics. Most recent are the findings of Anderson and Whitaker (2009), who report that nearly one in five American four-year-olds is obese and that the rate is even higher among certain groups. Like their counterparts who are concerned about childhood obesity, these researchers are troubled by their findings because of the many accompanying health problems associated with childhood obesity. True, there are many contributing factors associated with obesity, but there is little question that nutrition is central.

Why should nutrition be of concern to educators? Children's overall health and well-being aside, academic achievement is the primary concern. An ever-increasing body of research reveals that poor nutrition and obesity are two contributors to lower levels of student achievement (Florence, Asbridge, and Veugelers, 2008). The implication is that when educators support better nutrition, they also support increased academic performance (Satcher, 2008).

Fortunately, programs such as Action for Healthy Kids and We Can! are available to help children become healthier, thereby improving their academic performance and helping to ensure long, healthy lives. Much of the information supplied by organizations such as these is easily incorporated into existing classroom routines.

Indeed, each of the activities in this chapter is designed to enhance children's reading abilities while, at the same time, helping them to develop an understanding of the most recent *Dietary Guidelines for Americans* (2005). These guidelines, updated every five years by the Departments of Agriculture and Health and Human Services, provide authoritative recommendations for people two years and older about healthy eating habits and the positive effect they have on becoming and staying healthy. The overall goal is to endow children with enough information so that they can use literacy as a tool to become savvy consumers who know how to identify, purchase, and eat healthy foods. Figure 3.1 is an overview of the nutrition fitness activities and content literacy teaching strategies this chapter emphasizes.

	Shape Up! (MyPyramid for Kids)	Go, Slow, or Whoa? (different foods)	What's in This? (reading food labels)	Portion or Serving? (serving sizes)	What's the Trick? (advertising tricks)
Problem Perspective				X	
Concept Circle	X				
List, Group, Label		X			
External Text Structure			X		
Evaluating Images					X
Posing Problems				X	
Taking Action	X	X	X	X	X

▶ Figure 3.1 *Nutrition Fitness Lessons and Content Reading Skills*

Shape Up!

Description

Nutrition Fitness: Many different individuals, including nutritionists and dieticians, developed MyPyramid for Kids (see Appendix B) to help children understand the types of food available to them and how to eat a balanced diet (USDA, 2005). It is a visual representation that is based on the most current *Dietary Guidelines for Americans* (2005). The pyramid is also designed to help children understand that fueling their bodies with a balance of healthy foods enables them to have the energy they need both for physical activity and for learning.

Reading: One of the best ways for children to better understand and broaden their vocabularies is to categorize words (Vacca and Vacca, 2008). The concept circle is a tool designed to help children do just that. It encourages children to think about the relationships among a group of words by examining the attributes to determine what the words have in common. They then identify the overall category to which all belong.

FitLit Suggestions

Title	Author	Publisher/Year	Suggested Grade Levels
Bring Me Some Apples and I'll Make You a Pie	Robin Gourley	Clarion/2009	2–5
Chop, Simmer, Season	Alexa Brandenberg	Harcourt Brace & Company/1997	K–1
Good Enough to Eat: A Kid's Guide to Food and Nutrition	Lizzy Rockwell	HarperCollins Publishers/1999	K–2
Pizza at Sally's	Monica Wellington	Dutton Children's Books/2006	K–2
Still-Life Stew	Helena Clare Pittman	Hyperion Books for Children/1998	K–2

Connecting nutrition fitness and reading facilitates students' understanding of word relationships to better understand the various food groups shown on the food pyramid. Students also gain a heightened awareness of the many different foods that are classified within each group, leading them to see that they have many choices when considering what to eat for balanced, healthy meals.

Teaching Procedures

1. Select a text such as *The Edible Pyramid* (Leedy, 2007) that will provide students with information about the food pyramid.

2. Read and discuss the text with students in some manner (read-aloud, small group, guided reading, independent reading).

3. Create concept circles related to each food group. Here's how:

- Identify categories and words associated with them.

- Create circles for each set of words (see Figure 3.2).

- Think about how many examples you want to put into each circle and divide it accordingly.

- Above the circle, draw a line on which students can write the category that names the words shown in the circle.

4. Decide how you want to use the circles. If using with the whole class, put each on a visual large enough for all to see. You also need to think about where in the lesson the circles best fit. They are usually used to reinforce and extend understanding of vocabulary.

Classroom Voices

Carl wants his second graders to make healthy food choices daily. To that end, he selected *The Edible Pyramid* (Leedy, 2007) to read and discuss with his students. One of the main reasons he selected this book is that the author shows and explains the most recent graphic of the food pyramid (MyPyramid for Kids) published by the U.S. Department of Agriculture (2005). Now that his students have read and discussed the text, he wants to engage students using concept circles because he knows that classification is an excellent way for students to enhance their understanding of concepts—in this instance, the food pyramid.

He begins the lesson by calling the students together in the meeting area. Once they are settled, he holds up the text *The Edible Pyramid* and comments, "Yesterday, we read and discussed this book. Think for a minute, then turn to your neighbor to state one fact you learned." After giving students some time to share with partners, he solicits volunteers to share some ideas. "The pyramid shows different foods we should be eating," says Rachel. "And the different sizes tell how much of each we should have every day," Ben adds. Probing further, Carl asks, "So what are some of the food groups that different foods belong to?" In turn, different students volunteer the names of the various groups, and as they do, Carl refers back to the page in the text that shows that particular group. In so doing, Carl indirectly shows students how readers cross-check to verify information. Once having located the page associated with a specific food group, Carl also reviews the specific foods that are shown on the page.

Carl then comments, "Now that we have reviewed the book, I think you are ready to do some food classifying. Today, we're going to use some circles to help us classify. Watch me and I'll show you how." Carl displays the first concept circle (see Figure 3.2), stating, "Here's what I need to do to complete the circle. First, I have to look at the words that are in each part of the circle." He looks at the words and reads each aloud. He continues, "Second, I need to think about what all the foods have in common." Again, Carl stops and thinks aloud, "Hmmm. All of these foods name different kinds of bread." He then states, "My next step is to think of the name of the food group that all the foods belong to and write the label on the blank line." Once again, Carl thinks aloud, commenting, "All of these are kinds of bread and bread is made from grains. So I think the label is *grains*. I'm going to write the word *grains* on the line." Finally, Carl states, "I think I am correct, but I'll check with the book." He refers back to the appropriate page, showing students how to verify information with a reference.

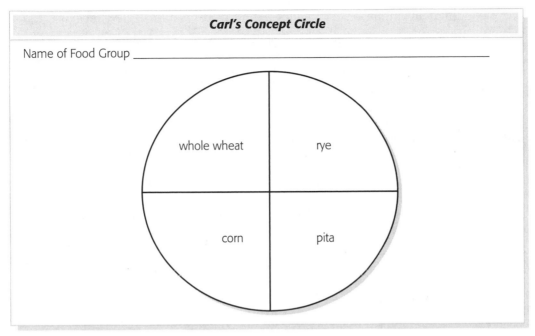

Carl's Concept Circle

Name of Food Group _____

whole wheat

rye

corn

pita

▶ Figure 3.2 *Carl's Concept Circle*

Having modeled the process, Carl states, "You are going to do exactly what I did when you read with me in small groups today. We'll do some of these circles as a group, and we'll use the book to check how well we did. Knowing about different foods and food groups puts you in a good position to be healthy eaters. So after we do some classifying, I'm also going to show you how you can keep track of what you eat at every meal."

Extensions

1. Consider using concept circles in other ways. For example, give students manipulatives (either word cards or picture cards) for various food groups along with a blank circle divided into however many sections you choose. State the name of the food group and have students find a representative example for each section of the circle. Once children are familiar with how the circles work, consider having them take on the role of teacher by creating circles for a partner or for the class.

2. Provide children with the MyPyramid form shown in Appendix B. Have them use it to keep a food log and to set both food and activity goals for succeeding days.

3. To enhance children's understanding of the pyramid, have them examine it more closely and pose questions such as those listed below.

Sample Question	Answer
Why are there steps along the left-hand side?	To remind people that they need to be physically active every day.
Why are the colored stripes different widths at the bottom of the pyramid?	To remind children that they need to choose more or fewer foods from the different groups. More foods need to be selected from those that are the widest.
Why do you suppose different colors are used for each group?	To remind children to eat all colors, or groups, every day. They should also eat some foods that have healthy oils.

Web Sites

www.mypyramidforkids.gov provides additional information aimed at children. It contains different forms children can download and use as reminders for eating healthy.

www.mypyramid.gov presents information that teachers and parents can use to further help themselves and children understand the pyramid.

www.kidnetic.com is another site geared for children. It contains games, recipes, and several informational articles about using nutrition to stay energized.

Tips for Professional Collaboration

School Nurse: Ask the school nurse to show children how to use the pyramid to plan balanced meals. The nurse could also have students analyze the breakfast or lunch meals provided at school.

Literacy Lessons to Help Kids Get Fit & Healthy

Go, Slow, or Whoa?

Description

Nutrition Fitness: As good as the MyPyramid for Kids is in helping to make clear different food groups, the U.S. National Heart, Lung, and Blood Institute went even further to help kids think about what they are eating. In 2005, the agency proposed classifying foods into three groups: Go, Slow, or Whoa. Go foods are foods that are appropriate to eat nearly any time and include items such as low-fat milk and low-fat yogurt. Slow foods are those that can be eaten, but not every day. Examples include pancakes and granola. Whoa foods are those we should eat only once in a while. They include French fries, cookies, and sausage. In other words, go foods are nutrient-dense, whereas whoa foods are calorie-dense. A detailed listing of the foods is available at the Web sites listed at the end of this activity.

Reading: Using higher-level thinking and one's own background knowledge are excellent ways for children to understand word relationships and to broaden their vocabularies. This is what *List-Group-Label* (Taba, 1967) is all about. After brainstorming words they know that relate to a given topic, children then group the words according to like attributes. The activity can play out in a couple of ways. Teachers can identify the main categories and encourage students to group the words accordingly. Alternately, the teacher might ask students to group the words according to their own categories and then provide reasons for their grouping strategies.

Integrating nutrition fitness and reading, Go, Slow, or Whoa? affords students an opportunity to use higher-level thinking, their own background knowledge, and classifying to learn about word relationships and nutrition simultaneously. Students learn that there are three main food categories and that many words can be classified into each. They also learn the implications of knowing about the three groups in order to eat balanced meals that leave them feeling full and satisfied.

FitLit Suggestions

Title	Author	Publisher/Year	Suggested Grade Levels
No More Cookies!	Paeony Lewis	Scholastic/2005	K–1
School Lunch	True Kelley	Holiday House/2005	2–4
Sweet Tooth	Margie Palatini	Scholastic/2004	1–4
The Vegetables We Eat	Gail Gibbons	Holiday House/2007	K–2
Yummy! Eating Through a Day	Lee Bennett Hopkins	Simon and Schuster Books for Young Readers/2000	K–2

Teaching Procedures

1. Tell students to think of different foods they like to eat.

2. Ask students to state words associated with the foods that came to mind and write each on a card.

3. In turn, display all cards in a chart holder or on the board ledge.

4. Show students a picture or model of a traffic light and ask them what the different colored lights represent.

5. Tell students that just as traffic lights signal drivers to go, slow down, or stop, so, too, can they be used to help people identify the foods they should eat. Green = go foods—foods that are good to eat every day. Yellow = slow foods—foods they can sometimes eat. Red = whoa foods—those that should make students stop and ask themselves, "Should I eat this?" These are foods that we can eat—but only once in a while.

6. Invite students to place each word into the go, slow, or whoa category, using the word cards they created.

7. Show students the U R What U Eat poster to check their categories (see Appendix B). Allow time for any necessary changes.

8. Based on their grouping, ask children how they can take action to make sure that they eat healthy foods.

Classroom Voices

Noticing what her fourth graders bring for snack and for lunch has led Julie to realize that they need a better understanding of food groups and how to make better choices. She sees the go, slow, whoa categories established by the U.S. Heart, Lung, and Blood Institute (2005) as a perfect way to accomplish this goal.

Students typically eat their morning snack at their tables while talking with one another. Once they are finished eating, Julie gathers them in the whole-group meeting area and begins her lesson. She states, "I noticed that all of you brought some different foods to eat for your snack today. Let's make some labels of what you brought today. You say the word and I'll write it on a card. I am then going to put each in our chart holder." One by one, students state what they brought. Julie then says, "Think for a minute if there are any other foods you like to eat. Once you have thought of it, go ahead and state it, and I'll write it on a card."

Next, Julie shows students the model traffic light she has brought in for this lesson. She comments, "This traffic light relates to the names of the foods I just wrote on the cards. Think about what you know about traffic lights, what you know about different foods, and how the two might be connected. When you are ready, turn to your neighbor and state your ideas." She pauses, giving students time to think and to share with one another. She then asks for a few volunteers to share their ideas. Manuel takes the lead, commenting, "Well, the green light means go and so does eating. I mean, you have to actually move by choosing the food and eating it." Susan adds, "I think that sometimes you get full so you stop, just like when my dad comes to a red light."

"You have the idea," Julie replies. "The traffic lights signal to us what action we should take in order to be safe. We either go, slow down, or stop." She continues, "Did you know that the same is true with different kinds of foods? Some foods we should eat all of the time." Pointing to the green light, Julie states, "These are called the *go foods.*" Pointing to the yellow light, she comments, "Some foods we eat are called *slow foods.* These are the foods that we can sometimes eat but we probably shouldn't eat them every day." Pointing to the red light, Julie states, "And *whoa foods* are foods that we should eat only every once in a while or on special occasions. They actually make us stop and ask ourselves, "Should I be eating this?"

Directing students back to the word cards, Julie comments, "Let's see if we can group these cards into go, slow, and whoa categories. Watch me as I do one for you." Julie selects one card and thinks aloud commenting, "Apple. I think that this is a go food because it is something I could eat every day to stay healthy." She places the card under a green circle. She continues, "This is exactly what you are going to do in your small groups today. I have made a traffic light for each group. What you are going to do is look at your words, talk about them, and come to a decision about where each belongs. You'll then have time to share with others in the class."

As students return to their tables, Julie gives each group four words and provides time for students to classify them. Once she sees that all are finished, she has each group report out, providing reasons for their groupings.

Finally, Julie comments, "Now let's take a look at the U R What U Eat chart to check our categories." She displays the chart and has students cross-check their selections with those shown on the chart. She also encourages students to rearrange their cards based on their new learning.

Julie concludes the lesson by stating, "It looks like you are beginning to develop an understanding of these different categories. Why do you think knowing about these categories might be important?" Without hesitating, Caroline responds, "I think you're trying to help us see that we should eat some foods all of the time and some not so much."

John adds, "I think that knowing about these will help me make better choices about what to bring for snack." Julie comments, "What you say makes a lot of sense to me. What I hear you saying is that you need to take action to do something about eating healthy. There are many different ways that you can keep track of your decisions and this form is one way to get you started." She displays the form using an overhead transparency (see Figure 3.3), explains that they will use it at school to track their snacks at school, and gives each student a copy to use for the week.

Taking Action for Go, Slow, Whoa Snacks

Name _____

Week _____

Directions:

1. Write what you brought for snack each day.

2. Place an "X" in the column that tells what kind snack it is.

3. At the end of the week, take a look at your chart. Rate yourself. Are you mostly a go, slow, or whoa kind of snacker? Make sure you set a goal for yourself for next week.

Day	Snack	GO	SLOW	WHOA
Monday				
Tuesday				
Wednesday				
Thursday				
Friday				
My goal for next week:				

▶ Figure 3.3 *Taking Action for Go, Slow, Whoa Snacks*

Extensions

1. A related understanding about categorizing foods has to do with food preparation. For example, a plain baked potato is a go food. Put a little butter on it and it becomes a slow food. Cut a raw potato into strips and fry them to make French fries, and it is now a whoa food. *Two Eggs, Please* (Weeks, 2003) is a perfect fit for helping children to develop this understanding, as it's all about preparing eggs in many different ways. Children can discuss which types of eggs (e.g., poached, scrambled, fried) belong to each group.

2. Pair children and give each couple one food item (either a picture or an empty food container), or let them select one. Have them discuss how to make the item a go, slow, and whoa food, and write their ideas on a chart labeled Go, Slow, Whoa. Provide time for all to share with the whole class. Consider combining all findings into a class chart and post as a reminder.

3. Challenge students to combine foods from the various food groups shown on the food pyramid (MyPyramid for Kids) to create a go food. For example, to create a go pizza, they could use half of an English muffin and some low-fat cheese. They could also add sauce to their taste.

Web Sites

www.playnormous.com/game_foodfury.cfm presents games at different grade levels designed to help children better understand the difference between go, slow, and whoa foods. There are teacher guides that provide several ideas for using the games.

www.nim.nih/gov/ offers parents a go, slow, whoa food chart that can be printed out and placed on the refrigerator.

www.kidshealth.org/kid/ provides children with a wealth of information about nutrition and other areas of wellness. Kid-friendly recipes are included. This site also has tabs for teens and parents.

Tips for Professional Collaboration

Media Specialist: Ask the media specialist to show children how to access *www.kidshealth.org/kid* and how to sign up for a free weekly newsletter.

What's in This?

Description

Nutrition Fitness: Nutrition facts labels show the nutrients, ingredients, and servings in a food product. It is one way to bring about meaningful application of the food groups and those that belong in the go, slow, and whoa categories. Although the USDA recommends that active children ages 4–8 need anywhere from 1,400 to 2,000 calories per day to stay healthy, the nutrition facts labels are calculated based on a 2,000 calories per-day adult diet. Children can nonetheless learn much from the label. They can be taught what the food contains (i.e., nutrients), how to identify the ingredients, what a "serving" constitutes, and how many calories each serving contains. Knowing how to read and interpret the label helps children ask and answer significant questions such as:

- Should I eat this food?

- If so, how much should I have at any one time?

- How does this food contribute to what I need to eat today?

Reading: Like the authors of narrative texts, authors of expository texts use a structure to organize the information they want to present to assist readers in gleaning the most important information. Many times they use external features to show the overall design of the text. A preface, table of contents, appendices, introductory or summary statements, headings, graphs, charts, and illustrations are all examples of external text features.

FitLit Suggestions

Title	Author	Publisher/Year	Suggested Grade Levels
Dog Biscuit	Helen Cooper	Farrar, Straus and Giroux/2008	K–2
Nutrition Anyone?	Kristin Petrie	ABDO Publishing Company/2004	2–5
Paula Deen's My First Cookbook	Paula Deen	Simon and Schuster Books for Young Readers/2000	K–3
Salad People and More Real Recipes: A New Cookbook for Preschoolers and Up	Mollie Katzen	Tricycle Press/2005	K–2
The Spatulatta Cookbook	Isabella and Olivia Gerasole	Scholastic/2007	3–5

Integrating nutrition fitness and reading, What's in This? gives students an opportunity to apply text structure to nutrition. Using the structure, they are taught how to locate specific information on a nutrition facts label and how to interpret what they discover. They are also taught how to use what they discover to make some decisions about whether to purchase and consume the product.

Teaching Procedures

1. Select an appropriate text such as *The Monster Health Book: A Guide to Eating Healthy, Being Active, and Feeling Great for Monsters and Kids* (Miller, 2006).

2. Gather empty food product containers (enough so that there is one for each partner group).

3. To help set the stage for reading nutrition labels, activate what students know about trading cards by asking questions such as, "What do you know about trading cards? What do you know about how authors write them?"

4. Read aloud the text to provide students with information about nutrition facts labels. Connect children's understanding about trading cards and text structure with nutrition facts labels.

5. Group children into partnerships. Provide each group with one food item and give them time to examine the nutrition facts label.

6. Pose questions about the labels (see Figure 3.4) to review and extend children's understanding of the nutrition facts labels.

7. Discuss how children can use what they know to take control of what they choose to eat. Distribute prompt card (see Figure 3.5) as a helpful reminder of what to look for and ask about foods.

Classroom Voices

Steven is a third grade teacher whose observations have helped him to see that the majority of his students enjoy reading and trading baseball cards. He decides to capitalize on their interests to teach them how to read nutrition facts labels. He begins the whole-class lesson by stating that he's noticed their interest in baseball cards. He then states, "I'm curious about what makes the cards so interesting to you." He pauses, giving time for students to volunteer their ideas. Lindsey comments, "Well, I like to look at the picture on the front of the card. It helps me to remember the name of the player shown on the card." Andrew chimes in with, "I like to see how well the person plays so I like to look at the back of the card that shows all of that information."

Taking Andrew's lead, Steven asks, "How is that information displayed? Is it broken out into categories?"

"It's always the same format," says Abby adding, "and it's a good thing because you know exactly where to look to compare one card to the next. You can look at the information and use it to decide if you want to keep or trade a card."

Acknowledging and extending Abby's comments, Steven says, "You have the idea, Abby. The authors of these cards are just like the authors who write informational books.

They use a specific structure to help you read the text—in this case, the statistics about the shown player. After reading the statistics, you can decide if you want to keep the card or get rid of it." He now begins to connect students' knowledge about trading cards to nutrition by asking, "Did you know that you can do the same thing when you are trying to decide what to eat?" Students' blank stares help Steven see he needs to elaborate, so he holds up a cereal box and says, "Just take a look at this cereal box. You see the picture of the cereal on the front, just like you see the picture of a player on the front of a baseball trading card. But take a look at this!" Pointing to the nutrition facts label, he adds, "Just like your baseball cards have the player's statistics on the back of the card to tell more about the player, so, too, does this package have statistics that tell more about the pictured food. The same structure is used to display the information on every food product. You can count on it. And just like your cards, if you know how to read it, you can make a decision about whether to keep it or get rid of it."

Steven then holds up a copy of *The Monster Health Book* (Miller, 2006) and says, "I'm going to use parts of this book to help you better understand how to read a nutrition facts food label. Listen and be ready to state at least one fact about the food label." He turns to pages 18 and 19 and reads them aloud as the students listen. Once finished, Steven reviews the nutrition facts label shown on page 19 by first soliciting ideas from students. He then reviews the six main points featured on the page.

Steven's Questions
1. How many servings are in your container? _____
2. How many calories are in each serving? _____
3. What kinds of nutrients are in your food? _____
4. What are the main ingredients in your food? _____

▶ Figure 3.4 *Steven's Questions*

Look and Ask Prompt Card	
Should you eat that food you are holding? Take a look at the nutrition facts label and answer these questions to help you decide!	
Look	**Ask**
Check the ingredients.	How much sugar has been added to this food?
Take a look at the number of servings.	How much of this food should I eat to get one serving?
Check out the calories and the nutrients.	Do the calories come from nutrients I need in order to be healthy?
What's your final answer: Eat it or Ditch it?	

▶ Figure 3.5 *Look and Ask Prompt Card*

The lesson proceeds with Steven giving students time to apply their learning by looking at different food product containers he has brought in. He pairs students and gives each partner one container saying, "Let's practice using what you know. You and your partner take a look at the nutrition facts label and be ready to answer some questions." Steven uses the six points about the nutrition label shown on page 19 to form his questions (see Figure 3.4). He asks the questions and gives students time to respond.

Steven brings the lesson to a close by stating, "Today you used both your knowledge of baseball cards and the ways authors write texts to help you learn something about reading nutrition facts labels. You learned that a specific text structure is used to write the labels and that the labels always provide the same type of information. You can use this information to help you make some decisions about the foods you eat. I made you this card to carry in your pocket so that you can remember how to look at and what to ask about a food that you are thinking about eating. You can take some action to control your eating habits." He distributes the card, inviting students to give it a try.

Extensions

1. Give children additional practice with using the *Look and Ask* prompt card by having them use it to examine additional food products. These could be foods from their own lunches, foods you have brought in to share with them, or foods served in the cafeteria.

2. Provide children with a food that does not have a label and have them create a label for it. Children can use a variety of sources such as *www.nutritiondata.com* to both construct their labels and verify the displayed information.

3. Building on children's understanding of food groups and/or grouping foods as go, slow, or whoa foods, have children use the information they gain from reading the nutrition facts labels to classify given food products.

Web Sites

www.nutritiondata.com provides an easy way to construct nutrition food labels. Simply enter the product name and hit the return key. A nutrition food label then appears showing the statistics for the food.

www.mypyramid.gov has an interactive tool titled My Pyramid Plan. Click on the button and it will take you to a page on which you can enter your demographic information. Hit submit and what you get is a page that shows how much food from each food group you should eat daily. Clearly, this is not a one-size-fits-all approach but rather is one tailored to individuals' unique differences.

www.busyteacherscafe.com offers a wealth of graphic organizers teachers can download and use to assist their teaching of text structure and more!

Tips for Professional Collaboration

Physical Education Teacher: Invite the physical education teacher to point out to students that different kinds of activities burn more or fewer calories. The teacher can also extend students' understanding of types of foods by pointing out the best type of foods to eat before or after a given activity.

Portion or Serving?

Description

Nutrition Fitness: Two terms that often get confused are *portion* and *serving*. A portion is the amount of food a person chooses to eat for any given meal or snack. A serving, on the other hand, is a measured amount of food, such as five pretzels or one cup of milk. In keeping with the current MyPyramid graphic display of the food groups, the nutrition facts labels show the serving size relative to household units (i.e., cups for fruits, vegetables, and milk; ounces for grains, meat, and beans).

Calling children's attention to the difference between the terms *portion* and *serving* is important. What we want children to understand is that they need to pay attention to the serving size in order to maintain a healthy weight. They also need to develop an understanding that eating a certain number of servings (i.e., portion) at one sitting will vary depending on their activity level. Understanding how to read the servings section of the nutrition facts label is critical.

Reading: Arousing curiosity is one way to anticipate what students might learn. It also enables students to think about what they might know about the topic at hand. They can also pose questions about what they are going to read, and read to discover answers. *Problem perspective* (Vacca and Vacca, 2008) is one way to arouse curiosity. In essence, the teacher presents a problem for students to solve and allots time for students to discuss it, form questions related to it, and think about possible solutions, before even taking a look at the text to be read. They then read the text in search of a resolution to their problem.

Connecting nutrition, fitness, and reading, Portion or Serving? encourages students to use literacy skills such as background knowledge, asking questions, and critical listening

FitLit Suggestions

Title	Author	Publisher/Year	Suggested Grade Levels
Bake You a Pie	Ellen Olson-Brown; Brian Claflin	Tricycle Press/2006	K–2
Harry Hungry!	Steven Salerno	Harcourt Brace & Company/2009	K–1
I Know an Old Lady Who Swallowed a Pie	Alison Jackson	Dutton Children's Books/1997	K–3
This is the Bread I Baked for Ned	Crescent Dragonwagon	Aladdin Paperbacks/1989	K–2
Wild Boars Cook	Meg Rosoff	Henry Holt and Company/2008	K–2

and thinking to learn more about nutrition, specifically the difference between the terms *portion* and *serving*. Students are also led to see why attending to serving sizes on nutrition facts labels is important and how they might take action to ensure that they eat the right amount of foods to maintain a healthy lifestyle.

Teaching Procedures

1. Select a text such as *True Lies* (Shannon, 1997) that you can use to model how to do the problem perspective. I have found this order to be helpful:

- Say something like, "Today I have a problem to solve. It's hidden in the story I am going to read to you."

- Read the story to the students. Ask questions such as "So what is the problem? How might it be resolved?"

- Provide time for students to discuss and share their ideas.

2. Focus the discussion on the difference between the terms *portion* and *serving* by reviewing the story and the author's resolution. Point out that there is a difference between a portion and a serving and that this is what the children in the story did not understand.

3. Ask students to share their ideas about the difference between the terms *portion* and *serving*. If needed, point out that portion is about eating however much of something one wants to eat at any one sitting. Serving is the recommended amount of any one food that one might consume at any given meal.

4. Show students a nutrition facts label and where information about serving size and number of servings per package is located.

5. Provide time for students to look at other food nutrition facts labels to determine the serving sizes and how many servings are contained in each package.

6. Discuss with children how they can take action to make sure that they are eating the correct number of servings.

7. On day 2, divide the class into small groups and give each group the same problem to solve. Provide each group with a copy of the problem and a list of the tasks they are to perform (see Figure 3.6).

Group Tasks

Here's what you need to do:

1. Silently read the problem.
2. Discuss the problem.
3. Pose any questions you might have about the problem.
4. Think about possible solutions.
5. Read the assigned text.
6. Report on your discussion.

▶ Figure 3.6 *Group Tasks*

Classroom Voices

In an effort to enhance children's healthy eating habits, Becky designs a lesson that helps her fifth-grade students understand the difference between the terms *portion* and *serving*. She believes that if students have to use higher-level thinking, they will better internalize the terms and the learning will have a lasting impact. She decides to use a variation of Problem Perspective to achieve her objectives.

Recognizing that she will need to model the entire process before she can expect students to successfully complete the activity on their own, Becky selects the story "One Cookie" from *True Lies* (Shannon, 1997) as a read-aloud to model for students. She begins by stating, "The title of this story is 'One Cookie,' and there is a major problem. Listen while I read it and see if you can figure out what the problem might be." When finished reading, Becky invites students to share their ideas. Some note that the major problem is that the mother doesn't trust her children. Others note that they think the children are telling the truth. The problem is that they ate a cookie large enough to feed at least two people!

Becky then poses another question. "So how do you think this problem might be resolved? Talk with your neighbor." She gives students time to discuss their ideas and then has some report out. She then reads the remainder of the story so that students can see how the author resolved the problem. She then hones in on explaining the difference between the terms *portion* and *serving*, commenting, "So as you hinted at earlier, the main problem in this story is that the two children did not appear to understand the difference between the terms *portion* and *serving*. What do you think the difference is? Think for a minute and share your thoughts with your neighbor." Becky then asks for volunteers to share their ideas. Rachel comments, "We think that serving is like eating a piece of a pie and a portion is eating the whole thing." Taking her lead and pointing to a displayed nutrition facts label, Becky asks, "Let's take a look at the word that the USDA authors used to create this label." She points to the words *serving size* and *servings per container*. Becky states, "It looks like *serving* is the word. But it still doesn't help to clarify the difference, so let me tell you. Actually, Rachel, you are on the right track. Portion is how much of something we eat at any one time. Serving is what the USDA recommends that we *should* eat at any one time. One of the best ways to keep fit is to pay attention to the serving size and the number of servings within one package. You might think that you are not overeating because a package looks small. It is only by reading the serving size and the number of servings per package that you will know for sure. Let's practice."

Becky then gives students some food wrappers and has students identify both serving size and number of servings per package. Once students have had this time to apply their understanding, she closes the lesson, stating, "Now that you know something about serving sizes, what do you think you can do to make sure you are eating the correct amounts?" Students offer several suggestions including making sure that they read the label and sharing part of a food with a friend if there is more than one serving. Becky concludes, "It sounds to me like you have a pretty good understanding of the term *serving.*" The following day, Becky engages students with a similar process but this time she shifts more of the learning onto students' shoulders by having them complete the process in small groups. She uses the directions shown in Figure 3.6 to that end.

Extensions

1. Mathematics is a natural when thinking about servings. Presenting children with problems such as "If there are 10 servings in the box and each serving is ½ cup, how many boxes of cereal will you need to feed 30 students?" Students can also use various nutrition facts labels from their favorite foods to construct additional problems for the class to solve.

2. Now that children know about serving sizes, give students time to apply their understanding by examining the contents of their lunches. Have students discuss what they might need to adjust if they have an item that contains several servings.

Web Site

www.nhlbi.nih.gov/health/public/obesity/wecon/eat-right/distortion.htm offers both online and PowerPoint slides that can be downloaded that show how food portions have changed over time. Also available is a PDF file that has serving size cards students can use as visual reminders of serving sizes and sample foods for each food group.

Tips for Professional Collaboration

Media Specialist: Ask the media specialist to help children use the Internet to discover how portion sizes have changed over time.

What's the Trick?

Description

Nutrition Fitness: Becoming nutritionally fit is challenging enough without the advertising techniques that are often used to entice children to focus on the package rather than the contents of the package. I'm saddened knowing adults responsible for creating such advertisements could very well be major contributors to childhood obesity and the many health issues that accompany it. Setting aside debates about just how much advertising influences purchases, the fact that companies have to be regulated to ward off false advertising seems proof that advertising plays a role in what children eat.

Fortunately for the children we teach, different entities such as the Media Awareness Network and the U.S. Department of Health and Human Services (publisher of the *Media-Smart* after-school program) go a long way in helping educators and interested others spread the word about advertising tricks to children (and adults). These organizations and the information they provide empower children by helping them become more knowledgeable and savvy consumers.

Reading: Helping children to think critically is an important part of being literate. And, as discussed in Chapter 1, when children are taught from a critical stance, they are taught to examine the reasoning behind why authors do what they do. They are taught that beliefs and perspectives guide one's actions. One way to get children to think and read critically is to guide them in the evaluation of commercial images. By showing children a cereal box that features a popular sports or movie star, for example, you can teach children to evaluate

FitLit Suggestions

Title	Author	Publisher/Year	Suggested Grade Levels
The Beastly Feast	Bruce Goldstone	Holt/1998	K–1
The Edible Pyramid	Loreen Leedy	Holiday House/2007	K–2
The Trouble With Cauliflower	Jane Sutton	Dial/2006	K–2
The Wild Bunch	Dee Lillegard	Putnam/1997	K–2
Yum Yum! What Fun!	Mara Bergman	Greenwillow/2009	K–1

why the image is placed on the box and how to look beyond it to the nutrition facts label to determine whether the product is worth purchasing.

Bringing nutrition fitness and reading together, What's the Trick? calls on students to use critical literacy skills to understand how advertisers promote food products. Children learn about two advertising tricks (bright colors and toys inside the box) and what they can do to look past the two techniques to make sure they are eating healthy foods.

Teaching Procedures

1. Identify at least two advertising tricks you want to make explicit to children (see the list of Web sites at the end of this activity to access the most commonly used techniques).

2. Bring in representative samples for students to examine.

3. Sort the packages according to the two advertising tricks each is intended to display.

4. Let children talk about their favorite foods for a minute or two, since seeing some of these foods is bound to get children talking.

5. Focus children's attention by asking them what they notice about the two different groups of food packages.

6. Discuss with students why they think the people who create food packaging might use bright colors and free toys.

7. Now that students are aware of two advertising tricks, ask them what they can do to avoid being tricked in the future.

Classroom Voices

Shannon has decided that the best way to help her first graders become more aware of how advertisers trick them into buying foods is to bring in a variety of food packages that show two different advertising tricks: flashy advertising and free toys or prizes. She displays them along the chalk ledge in two distinct groups and invites children to join her to discuss the items.

Shannon doesn't have to ask for volunteers! Students immediately are taken with the different packages and offer unsolicited comments. Shannon expected that this is how the children would respond so she provides them with a little time to share their ideas.

Shannon signals children to get their attention and comments, "You'll notice that I have put these packages into two different groups. Why do you suppose I did that?"

Bill responds, "Some have toys in them! I like the toys in that cereal. I've collected all of them." Brenda replies, "I like the colors! That's why I have my mom buy THAT cereal (she points to signal which she is talking about.)" Juan adds, "I like the toys I get!" After a few more students add their ideas, Shannon proceeds, stating, "I think you have the two categories I was thinking about but let's check. All of these in this first group have bright, flashy colors. Those in the second group have toys inside." She asks for a volunteer to point to each and instructs the others to say "Yea" if the package fits the category and "Nay" if it doesn't.

Shannon continues, "You did a very good job of identifying the categories. But I have another question for you. Why do you think that people who create the food packages use bright colors and toys? Think for a bit and when you are ready, share with us." While Shannon's students are most often eager to share ideas, this question appears to have them stumped. Hearing no responses, Shannon comments, "I think you might know why colors and toys are used but cannot tell me because of the way I asked the question. Let me give it another try. When you looked at these packages, what did you notice?" That does it! Students have no trouble stating that they noticed the colors and the toys and that they like both! Shannon proceeds, "Exactly right! And you are doing *exactly* what those people want you to do. But come closer! I have a secret to tell you!" Students huddle together and lean in to hear Shannon whisper, "They have tricked you! They used colors and toys to get you to like something that may not be the best food for you to eat." She then motions students to sit back and continues the lesson talking in a normal volume.

"Now that you know these two tricks, what do you think you can do to make sure that the food is not only colorful but good for you?" Most students agree that they can ask their parents, and Shannon supports their ideas. "Yes, asking a knowledgeable adult is an excellent idea. Pointing to the nutrition facts label on one of the packages, she states, "This is just the label you and your parents can read to make some decisions about whether or not the food is good for you. This label is what is most important on the package." She reads through one label to provide students with an overview.

Shannon brings the lesson to a close, stating, "So how about it? Instead of being tricked, how about if you trick the advertisers by having your parents check out the label before you ask them to buy you the food?" All students signal agreement by nodding their heads. Shannon smiles. She knows that they will give it a try but she also knows that changing their behavior will take considerable effort. Advertising gimmicks are deeply ingrained in society.

Extensions

1. To make this lesson more sophisticated, ask students to compare and contrast different packages, noting their similarities and differences. Then have children visit *www.pbskids. org/dontbuyit/advertisingtricks* and use it to identify any advertising tricks that are evident for the various products.

2. Pose a question such as "Should fast food companies be permitted to use advertising tricks to sell their products?" and invite students to debate it. Encourage them to use different sources (e.g., books, magazines, reports, Internet) to locate supporting evidence.

Web Sites

www.nutritionandmedia.org shows several suggestions for teaching children to be aware of advertising tricks. (The site is primarily geared toward adults.)

www.pbskids.org/dontbuyit/advertisingtricks shares kid-friendly information about the tricks advertisers use to get children to buy their products.

www.justthink.org provides children with terms that advertisers use in the media.

Tips for Professional Collaboration

Media Specialist: Encourage the media specialist to use the PBS Web site listed above to have children investigate and report out on additional advertising tricks.

CHAPTER 4

Integrating
SOCIAL FITNESS
AND LITERACY

Most classroom teachers already know what brain researcher Eric Jensen (2006) and psychologist Daniel Goleman (2006) attempt to better elucidate: the classroom is as much social as it is academic. Teachers know that children who are able to get along with others and develop friendships perform better academically because they sense that they belong. It is just this sense of belonging that teachers strive to create in their classrooms from the very first day of school and throughout the school year. Some incorporate friendship songs into the daily routine whereas others arrange student desks into small pods of four. Each pod is then responsible for caring for a geranium placed in the middle of the pod. Still others intentionally design lessons to teach students how to interact with one another. Regardless of the way different teachers create a sense of belongingness, their firsthand experience demonstrates that social skills such as how to get along with others, how to form friendships, and how to appreciate similarities and differences among individuals are all "people skills" that need to be taught and nurtured.

Just as with physical and nutritional fitness, then, social fitness needs time in the school day for not only does being socially connected enhance academic performance, it also reduces illness, absenteeism, and discipline problems (Jensen, 2006). Without a doubt, to be successful in and out of school, children need experiences that will enable them to learn how to communicate with one another. I wholeheartedly agree with the statement by the Association for Supervision and Curriculum Development (ASCD) Commission on the Whole Child that "children of all ages must have broad-based experiences to develop both the skills and knowledge that prepare them for a successful future" (2007, 11).

The good news is that reading and the other language arts promote social fitness in authentic, meaningful contexts. Think of the many times, for example, when teachers group children together to read and discuss a text. The discussion can be successful only if children know how to talk with one another and how to acknowledge one another's ideas. Children learn to include all members in a discussion and accept a range of opinions. They also have to learn social skills such as turn-taking, using nonverbal cues, and active listening.

	Acts of Kindness	True Friends	Appreciating and Including Others	Manners, Please	Don't Be Bullied
Brainstorming		x			
Semantic Feature Analysis				x	
Guided Reading Procedure	x				
Intra Act					x
Questioning the Author			x		
Alternate Perspectives					x
Evaluating Images			x		
Taking Action	x	x	x	x	x

▶ Figure 4.1 *Social Fitness Lessons and Content Reading Skills*

Helping children develop these social skills and attend to social fitness is what this chapter is all about. Each activity is designed to enhance children's reading abilities while simultaneously helping them develop an understanding of social fitness. Figure 4.1 is an overview of the social fitness activities and content literacy teaching strategies this chapter highlights.

Acts of Kindness

Description

Social Fitness: Understanding how to interact with others in ways that engender a sense of belonging and acceptance is a social skill children need to learn. One way to bring about this understanding is to help children understand how to treat others with kindness. Opening doors for one another, encouraging others to participate by smiling at them and offering compliments are all ways of showing kindness. As children grow in their understanding of what it means to be kind, they are sure to generate many ways to perform acts of kindness.

Reading: One benefit of living in the information age is the availability of vast amounts of information within minutes of asking a question. This inundation creates a need for readers to read a piece of text, grasp main points of that text, and then organize these with connecting details. The Guided Reading Procedure (Manzo, 1975) goes even further by expecting students to use their memory and retelling skills as a precursor to designating main points to organize and reflect upon.

Connecting social fitness and reading, Acts of Kindness facilitates students' using many literacy skills (e.g., reading, listening, speaking, writing, and viewing) to learn about socially acceptable ways of showing kindness to others. In so doing, students learn how treating others with kindness can enrich their lives both in and out of school.

FitLit Suggestions

Title	Author	Publisher/Year	Suggested Grade Levels
Brendan and Belinda and the Slam Dunk!	Anne Rockwell	Harper Collins Publishers/2007	K–1
I Like Your Buttons	Sarah Marwil Lamstein	Boyds Mills Press/1999	K–2
Let's Eat!	Ana Zamorano	Scholastic/1996	K–2
We Are Extremely Very Good Recyclers	Lauren Child	Dial Books for Young Readers/2009	K–2
Whopper Cake	Karma Wilson	Candlewick Press/2007	K–2

Teaching Procedures

1. Select a text such as *Kindness Is Cooler, Mrs. Ruler* (Cuyler, 2007) that introduces students to ways they can contribute to a caring and collaborative community.

2. Before reading the text, introduce the topic of kindness using a whole-group discussion about what it means to show kindness. Use a semantic map or matrix large enough for all to see to visually represent the discussion.

3. Model the guided reading procedure (GRP) using the beginning of the text (pp. 1–8) as a way to introduce the concept of kindness toward others.

- Set the purpose for your reading.

- Read the portion of the text aloud.

- Turn the book facedown on your lap.

- Think aloud a retelling of this portion, recording all you can remember on the whiteboard.

- Ask students if they recognize what you may have forgotten or remembered incorrectly.

Literacy Lessons to Help Kids Get Fit & Healthy

- Verify the retelling by returning to the text.

- Summarize the retelling in sequenced bulleted main points.

- Compare concepts from the semantic web to those in the bulleted outline.

4. Use the GRP in small groups by giving each group a portion of the text to read (i.e., jigsawing), and by having each group create an outline for their portion of text.

5. Bring all outlines together to form one complete outline of the text. Compare it to the semantic web created at the beginning of the lesson.

6. Informally assess students' understanding of the text by having them provide a brief response that enables them to apply what they learned about acts of kindness. They can also use this response to show how they will take action to be kind to others.

Classroom Voices

Following another recess filled with tattling and hurt feelings, Andrea calls her second graders together for a class meeting. She explains that the purpose of their meeting is to discuss what has been going on at recess. After several comments, including Patrick's description of how he was ignored when he requested to join in a four-square game and Betsy's story of missing out on jumping rope due to kids "hogging all the jump ropes," Andrea tells students that incidents like these show her that students are ready to learn more about kindness. She holds up the book *Kindness Is Cooler, Mrs. Ruler* (Cuyler, 2007), commenting, "This is the perfect book to help you learn more about kindness. You're going to be reading parts of it today and I am going to show you how."

She begins the lesson by asking, "What does it mean to show kindness? Who shows you kindness in your life? How do people show kindness to one another? Think and then share your ideas with your neighbor." As students discuss and volunteer their ideas with the whole group, Andrea creates a semantic map on chart paper. She will use this semantic map repeatedly throughout the lesson as the class compares their concept of kindness to those of the author's in *Kindness Is Cooler, Mrs. Ruler*. Andrea states, "This semantic map helps us set our purpose for reading *Kindness Is Cooler, Mrs. Ruler.* As we read this story in small groups today, we'll see if the author thinks of kindness the way we do. I'll get you started with your reading by reading aloud the first few pages and demonstrating what you'll do in small groups to read the part of the book assigned to your group." Andrea continues, modeling the guided reading procedure. She reads aloud pages 1–8 of the text. Stopping and placing the book facedown on her lap, she explains that in order to understand the author's message, it's sometimes necessary to stop and reflect on what has happened after reading a few pages. She uses a think-aloud to retell the first portion of the text, writing on the board each part she remembers, so that all can see.

As she rereads her retelling, Andrea asks students if they notice anything missing or any parts of the retelling that didn't happen as she remembered. She uses the previously read text and illustrations to address any needed clarifications. Andrea then creates a bulleted outline of phrases following the plot sequence of the story. Using this outline and the semantic web, Andrea asks students, "Do you think the author thinks about kindness the way we do? This is the question we'll continue asking in our small-group reading today. We'll then discuss our answers when we come together as a whole class. You are going to use the very same procedure I used to read your text. I'll be there to help you." Once all students have met with her in small groups to read their portion of the text, Andrea brings the whole class together to share their discoveries. She then reads aloud the concluding pages of the book. Finally, she asks students to orally retell the ending and decide what they should add to the story outline.

Andrea concludes the lesson commenting, "You've now had some time to think about kindness and what the author of this book thinks about kindness. Remember that one of our purposes for reading was to see how the author's ideas compared to ours, so here's your question: What is similar about how we think about kindness and how the author thinks about kindness? Think for a minute, then turn and share with your neighbor." Once students have had some time to talk to one another, Andrea states, "It sounds to me as if you have several ideas about how you can show kindness. Some of these you already knew. Some you learned from the author. Now it's time for you to use what you know to take action." She asks students to draw or write on a sticky note something they will do to show kindness to someone in the classroom and on the playground. Andrea provides time for students to share their notes. She then assembles them on a chart large enough for all to see. Andrea then suggests that students challenge themselves for the next month by removing a sticky note for each act of kindness they complete.

Extensions

1. Provide ways that students can catch one another being kind and show appreciation for the kind acts others bring to their lives. Teaching students how to write informal thank-you notes may stir them into action!

2. Bring the classroom community together for a common kindness goal, such as collecting toys for the disadvantaged, taking care of a local park, or taking part in a one-day event such as volunteering at a shelter.

3. Challenge students to identify kind acts being done by others in their community, school, church, or other organization and share them with the class to provide other ideas for ways they can take action with kindness.

Web Sites

www.actsofkindness.org/ provides ideas for encouraging kindness in classrooms of all ages, and includes a place where kids can share stories of their own acts of kindness.

www.kidscare.org/ hosts a wealth of ideas for children to begin developing a spirit of volunteerism and social responsibility, including a project of the month.

www.readwritethink.org/lessons/lesson_view.asp?id=259 presents an integrated primary-level lesson plan inspired by Dr. Martin Luther King, Jr.'s call for kindness.

Tips for Professional Collaboration

Physical Educator: Invite the physical educator to provide students with time to discuss how they show kindness when participating in physical activities. Consider labeling a chart "Showing Kindness During Physical Activities" and brainstorming with students what to put on the list. Once the list is complete, review it periodically either before or after the day's physical activities.

True Friends

Description

Social Fitness: Ask different people what friendship means and you are likely to get a lot of different responses. Nonetheless, most agree that friends are those who show genuine concern for one another and have others' best interest at heart. Learning how to be a friend can be difficult for children to understand. For example, we might hear a child say something like, "I'll be your friend if you give me your apple." A comment such as this helps to show that children need to be taught that friendship is a caring, interpersonal relationship rather than one centered on attaining any kind of material reward. Learning how to develop friendships is an important part of life.

Reading: Brainstorming is one way of showcasing many of the perspectives and experiences that contribute to students' definitions of a concept, while likely enlarging and enhancing their personal definitions through exposure to one another's ideas. It is also a way to activate students' thinking prior to reading, thereby increasing interest and comprehension. One important component of brainstorming is accepting all ideas.

Connecting social fitness and reading, True Friends affords students an opportunity to use literacy skills (speaking and listening) and their background knowledge to learn more

FitLit Suggestions

Title	Author	Publisher/Year	Suggested Grade Levels
Chicken Soup by the Heart	Esther Hershenhorn	Simon & Schuster Books for Young Readers /2002	K–1
The Friendly Four	Eloise Greenfield	Harper Collins Publishers/2006	K–2
The Greatest Story Never Told: The Babe and Jackie	Ray Negron	The Bown Press/2008	K–2
Help! A Story of Friendship	Holly Keller	Philomel Books/2007	3–5
Toot Toot Zoom!	Phyllis Root	Greenwillow Books/2009	K–2

about friendship. It also sets them up for reading success by providing time for them to think and talk with others before and after reading. Students also use social skills to engage with the text and their partner. Finally, True Friends enables students to use yet another literacy skill (writing) to show how they will take action to develop friendships.

Teaching Procedures

1. Select a text that introduces students to ways they can contribute to a caring and belonging community. *Willoughby and the Lion* (Foley, 2007) is a fitting example.

2. Determine at which points you will stop to engage students in making connections to their own lives.

3. Pair students according to similar achievement levels and gather enough books about friendship so that each pair can have one book.

4. Conduct a brainstorming session, recording every idea that surfaces in the group on an overhead or large chart paper. Keep this visual display posted throughout the lesson.

5. Provide time for students to pair up to read their assigned books in a manner comfortable to them (e.g., choral reading, alternating pages). Also instruct students to create a brainstorming page using the same procedure for the original whole-group brainstorming.

6. Ask them next to compare their list to the one produced as a whole class and to circle new ideas that are not on the class list.

7. Add to the original brainstorming list the circled ideas the partners share with the whole group.

8. Ask students to take action in their own lives by using what they know to form and maintain true friendships.

Classroom Voices

It's the beginning of a new school year and Karen has already noticed the loneliness of her third-grade students who have just moved into the neighborhood and are new to the school. Believing strongly in the influence of social fitness in learning, Karen takes action to help them work through their loneliness by planning a mini-unit about friendship. For today's lesson, she decides to use brainstorming as a way to engage all students in understanding the importance of true friendships in their lives, and how to be a true friend to others. She will also read aloud to them and partner students for reading texts she has strategically selected for each pair.

Karen begins her lesson with an interactive read-aloud of *Willoughby and the Lion* (Foley, 2007), stopping periodically at predetermined points aimed at helping students connect the ideas in the text to their own lives. Stopping on page 5, she asks, "What would you wish for if you were asked to wish for the most wonderful thing of all?" Following their opportunity to think, pair up, and share with the group, Jean and Jimmy proclaim, "We think it would be cool to wish for a huge playground with monkey bars connecting everything and a pool to jump in from the top!" After acknowledging their idea, she asks them all to compare their ideas to the author's, which are expressed through Willoughby's wishes, and continues with the read-aloud.

Following the interactive read-aloud, Karen begins a brainstorming session by asking, "How do you know you have a true friend in your life? We can start with how we think the author might answer this question and then move on to some of your own ideas." Karen emphasizes the value in *every* idea that students offer by writing *all* ideas on the overhead transparency. She notes to herself those comments that show students' attention to the value of friendships, attributes of true friends, and the feelings students have about their personal friendships.

The following day, Karen briefly reviews yesterday's lesson and then transitions to the next part of her unit. She strategically pairs students with similar achievement levels, shows them the book they will be reading, and gives them time to find a spot in the room where they feel comfortable reading. Students are familiar with this type of reading activity. Nonetheless, before they begin, Karen offers a few reminders, stating, "Remember that you both need to agree on how you want to read this text, taking turns or reading the book in unison. Also, when you have finished reading your book, please use the plain paper on the front table to record your brainstormed list of ideas about friendship as prompted by the author of your book. I'll leave our class brainstorm list up from yesterday to remind you of our original question and as a reminder to write down *every* idea you or your partner think of." She continues, "Once you have made your list, please compare it to our class list. Circle any ideas on your list that are not shown on our class list from yesterday." Students then begin reading and brainstorming while Karen hones in on students who need additional reading and writing support. Once all are finished, Karen instructs students to bring their books and lists to the meeting area to share their circled items and adds them to the whole class brainstorm list.

Karen concludes the lesson by rereading the brainstormed list aloud, noting that the list represents their different perspectives and those of various authors. Karen returns to *Willoughby and the Lion*, rereads the last four pages, and takes out the coin setting in the back cover of the book. She asks, "Why do you think the author embossed these pictures and words on the coin? What does that tell us about the author's ideas about true friendship?" After listening to students' ideas, Karen comments, "So now that you have all these ideas about what it means to be a friend, you can take some action by using these coins to write what you can do to be a true friend and what you need from others for a true friendship." She distributes the coins (see Figure 4.2) and provides students with time to write their ideas.

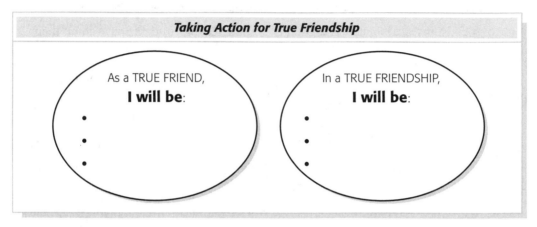

▶ Figure 4.2 *Taking Action for True Friendship*

Extensions

1. Encourage students to talk to their parents and/or siblings about the true friends in their lives and what makes these friendships important.

2. Consider ways to help students get to know one another, providing opportunities to cultivate true friendships. Using pen pals within the classroom or between classrooms in the same grade level may help students discover local friends they've never known.

3. Direct students' attention to friendships found in a wide variety of stories, novels, news articles, comics, their favorite movies, and so on and determine characteristics the characters' friendships share and those that make the friendships unique.

Web Sites

www.atozkidsstuff.com/friendship.html provides a wealth of ideas for teaching children about friendship and a lot more! Activities are aimed at toddlers, preschool, or elementary age children. Click on the tab that corresponds to the age level you want to explore.

www.goodcharacter.com/YCC/BeingFriends.html offers a *Being Friends* teaching guide that can be used with or without the *Being Friends* video in the *You Can Choose!* video series.

www.dltk-kids.com/crafts/friendship/mwreath.htm gives detailed instructions for making a friendship wreath with the whole class. Additional ideas are provided for home activities, too.

Tips for Professional Collaboration

Physical Educator: Ask the physical educator to provide students with time to discuss and show how they can show friendship when playing a team sport.

Appreciating and Including Others

Description

Social Fitness: Yet another social skill students need to acquire is accepting and including individuals who might look and behave different than they do. Just as books cannot be judged by their covers, neither can individuals. We want children to understand that what's beneath the surface is what is most important. All individuals, however different they might look or behave, long to be accepted for who they are and to be invited to participate in group activities.

Reading: Comprehension requires a questioning mind, one that actively seeks to construct meaning of a text by using the author's words and one's own background relative to the text at hand. Questioning the Author (QtA) (Beck, McKeown, Hamilton, and Kucan, 1997)) is

FitLit Suggestions

Title	Author	Publisher/Year	Suggested Grade Levels
Dancin' in the Kitchen	Wendy Gelsanliter, Frank Christian	Farrar, Straus and Giroux/1998	K–3
Foo, the Flying Frog	Belle Yang	Candlewick Press/2009	K–2
The Girl Who Wanted to Dance	Amy Ehrlich	Candlewick Press/2009	2–3
No Baloney!	Tammi Sauer	Collins/2009	K–1
Pebble: A Story About Belonging	Susan Milford	Dutton Children's Books/2007	4–6

a comprehension strategy that guides students in developing this questioning mind. It calls on students to consider an author's intentions for writing specific information and whether or not the author succeeds in communicating with the reader. It is a form of critical reading in that students must evaluate the author's intent for including and excluding specific information.

Combining social fitness and reading, Appreciating and Including Others helps students use critical listening and reading to learn more about appreciating likenesses and differences among individuals. They also learn what they can do to show their acceptance of others.

Teaching Procedures

1. Select a text that presents opportunities to consider an author's overall message, choice of words, ideas supporting his or her message, or patterns used within the text. *And Here's to You!* (Elliott, 2009) is an excellent primary-level example.

2. Read the text carefully, placing sticky notes to indicate places in the text that will elicit discussion regarding the following:

• What the author is trying to say (the overall message)

- What the author is intending to mean through his or her choice of words

- What the author has left out and why

- Whether the author is clear in his or her communication of ideas

- How the author encourages the reader to connect to the text and make inferences

3. Introduce the general topic of the lesson, in this case appreciating others, connecting it to prior learning whenever possible.

4. Guide students through an interactive read-aloud, stopping at the predetermined places in the text that you previously identified. Elicit responses from students using techniques such as think-pair-share, partner nominations (i.e., choosing a partner's response for sharing with others), and gestured response (e.g., thumbs up, thumbs down).

5. As a class, determine the author's overall message, and ask students to think about how it applies in their own lives through an activity such as the *Take Action Treasure Hunt* (see Figure 4.4).

Classroom Voices

Rhonda recalls that her kindergarten students have been learning about bar graphs and that they just recently created a graph to show student and teacher characteristics. She recognizes that this graph is a perfect way to start a lesson aimed at helping students appreciate the similarities and differences among individuals. Her overall goal is to help students be accepting of others. Having just learned about Questioning the Author (QtA), she decides to give it a try using the book *And Here's to You!* (Elliott, 2009). However, instead of having her students read the text, she will have them listen to it and apply the *QtA* techniques to their listening. She uses the procedures noted above to prepare. She also moves the students' graph to the whole-group area so that she and the students can refer to it as necessary.

Rhonda calls her students to the meeting area. After settling in, Rhonda points to the graph and asks, "What can you tell me about this graph we made last week?" Always eager to share, Sunny pipes up with, "We were adding up all the people that wore sneakers, and all the people that wore boots, and all the people that wore fancy shoes to school." Other students take Sunny's lead, offering their ideas including hair color, hair length, clothing, and height. Rhonda then turns the students' attention to the front cover of *And Here's to You!* (Elliott, 2009), explaining that the class graph shows how students and teachers can be similar and different, ". . . much like David Elliott shows using animals and others in his book."

Recalling students' enjoyment of hearing a story without interruptions, Rhonda reads aloud the entire text, getting into the rhythm of the poetry as the children enjoy the colorful pictures and the repetitive verse. Once finished, Rhonda comments, "Now that you've heard the whole story, we are going to take another look at it so that we can really think about what David Elliott wrote and how it might relate to our graph here." She proceeds to reread through page four, stops, and asks, "So if we were to make a graph showing the characteristics of birds, what does David Elliott believe we should include?" After pausing to give students time to think and to consider the illustration, Rhonda states, "Turn to your shoulder partner to share your ideas." Rhonda asks for volunteers to share by nominating their partners' ideas. Hunter takes her up on her offer, stating, "Ellie thinks maybe we could add the noises they make." "Yes, that seems like a great idea, Ellie! You noticed how the text

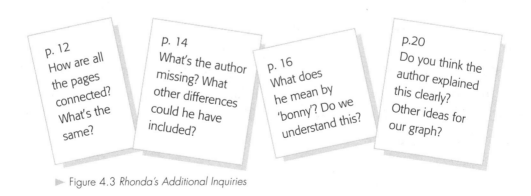

▶ Figure 4.3 *Rhonda's Additional Inquiries*

Literacy Lessons to Help Kids Get Fit & Healthy

mentions those birds that 'Whooo' and those that 'Cock-a-doodle-doo'," Rhonda replies, relieved the students are catching on.

"Before we read any further," Rhonda states, "we should probably be sure we understand what Mr. Elliott means by this phrase that he uses on every page, 'Here's to the…'. Do you notice that he uses this in the title, too? What do you think he means by these words?" Rhonda is glad she's included this clarification question, as the students' facial expressions seem quizzical. Maggie breaks the silence, suggesting, "I think he means that he's glad those animals are around." Hank adds, "I heard my grandpa say that at Thanksgiving dinner. He said, 'Here's to the family and good food!'" Rhonda adds, "That makes me think the author wants us to *appreciate* these animals that he's writing about and all the wonderful things about them. Would you agree?" Many heads respond nodding their heads yes.

After reading through the next few pages, Rhonda stops on page 12 and asks, "So what is the author saying is similar about all bugs? Let's take a moment to think-pair-share this one." Rhonda then calls on a few pairs to hear their responses, and confirms them by cross-checking with the printed text. She follows this by posing a related question, "Now that we know what Mr. Elliott thinks is similar about all bugs, let's think-pair-share to figure out what he thinks may be different among various bugs." Again, students respond quickly and determine several differences, such as bugs that have wings and those that don't, bugs that sting, and those that make honey. Students are now very engaged with the Questioning the Author comprehension strategy and use critical thinking to respond to Rhonda's additional inquiries (see Figure 4.3).

Rhonda closes the lesson asking, "So what do you think David Elliott wants you to learn from his book?" Most students comment that he wants them to appreciate others, both for the similarities they share and for the differences that make them unique. "I think you are correct," Rhonda comments. "There's just one more thing we need to do. We need to use what we know to show others that we appreciate their differences. We want to make sure that everyone is accepted for who they are. So we're going to go on a taking-action treasure hunt!"

Here's to ME!

▶ Figure 4.4 *Taking-Action Treasure Hunt*

Directions: Create a 2 x 4 grid titled "Here's to Me!" Have students choose one characteristic to write or draw about in each box. Encourage students to mimic Elliott if they're in need of ideas, thereby including not only aspects of their appearance, but things they are good at doing, and things they enjoy. Then, direct students to share their grid with others in the class, signing their initials on a fellow student's box when they find they have something in common with him or her. Finish the activity by posing, "What unique characteristic did you learn to appreciate about someone in our community?"

Extensions

1. Seat students in a circle, each with their own large index card. Once students have their names written on the top, pass the index cards to the right. As the cards are passed around, students write one phrase or sentence telling something specific they like about the person. Students can keep these cards as a reminder of what others appreciate about them.

2. Use Venn Diagrams within literature studies to help students identify characteristics of themselves that are similar to and different from those of main characters they're reading about. Doing so can help children continue to develop and appreciate their own identity.

Web Sites

www.readwritethink.org/lessons/lesson_view.asp?id=890 provides a lesson using Todd Parr's picture book *It's OK to Be Different*. The lesson incorporates online publishing tools and both individual and group exploration of personal characteristics.

www.pbs.org/parents/arthur/activities/diversity.html gives a number of lesson ideas on diversity appreciation and understanding.

www.pbs.org/kcts/preciouschildren/diversity/index.html is a site dedicated to teaching activities and related readings promoting diversity in the classroom. Some topics include dealing with insensitivity to physical, racial, or ethnic differences and teaching young children to resist bias.

Tips for Professional Collaboration

School Nurse: Ask the school nurse to teach children more about the range of body types that exist among children of any given grade. Lead them to conclude that being different is natural.

Manners, Please!

Description

Social Fitness: Knowing how to behave in socially accepted ways (i.e., manners) is an acquired skill that matures with time. While most adults unconsciously use social niceties to engage with one another, children tend to be uninhibited. Take, for example, the child who took a close look at a teacher I know and, having studied her face asked, "Were you pretty when you were young?" Rather than scold the child, we recognize that the child has yet to learn that some comments are not socially acceptable and we seize the opportunity

FitLit Suggestions

Title	Author	Publisher/Year	Suggested Grade Levels
Are You Quite Polite? Silly Dilly Manners Songs	Alan Katz	Margaret K. McElderry Books/ 2006	K–4
Don't Forget Your Etiquette!: The Essential Guide to Misbehavior	David Greenberg	Farrar, Straus and Giroux/2006	K–3
Don't Lick the Dog: Making Friends With Dogs	Wendy Wahman	Henry Holt and Company/2009	K–2
Emily's Magic Words: Please, Thank You, and More	Cindy Senning-Post	Collins/2007	K–1
Smelly Locker: Silly Dilly School Songs	Alan Katz	Margaret K. McElderry Books/ 2008	3–5

to teach him just that. How important it is, then, for children to learn socially accepted behaviors, for if they do not, they will be seen as social misfits.

Reading: Using background knowledge about known words to help them learn additional associated words is an excellent way for children to understand word relationships, thereby broadening their vocabulary. The *semantic feature analysis* (SFA) (Pittleman, Heimlich, Berglund, and French, 1991) is an activity that draws on students' understandings and extends them. Using a visual display, students examine how words are alike and different and how many different words are related to a given vocabulary concept.

Joining social fitness and reading, Manners, Please! helps children to better understand socially accepted behaviors (manners) by developing and using a vocabulary associated with them. Students then use their new understandings when interacting with others in different contexts (e.g., classroom, cafeteria, playground, home).

Literacy Lessons to Help Kids Get Fit & Healthy

Teaching Procedures

1. Identify a vocabulary concept you want to help students better understand and a text that exemplifies words or ideas relating to the concept. *M Is for Mischief: An A to Z of Naughty Children* (Ashman, 2008) is a good example for helping children learn about the terms *naughty* and *nice* and relating them to appropriate behaviors (manners).

2. Decide whether you will determine all words that closely relate to the concept or would prefer that your students come up with related words. (This will depend on your students' prior knowledge of the concept being taught.)

3. Create a semantic feature analysis (SFA) grid, using as many columns and rows as needed to thoroughly understand the concept (see Figure 4.5). Here's how:

- Place the main concept(s) or ways the concept is applied in the heading(s) across the top of the grid.

- Place the related words down the left side of the grid.

4. Explain and demonstrate how to use the SFA:

- Examine the word relationships.

- Place a (+) in each cell to indicate which words share a common feature and a (-) if there is no relationship.

5. Once students show understanding, provide each small group with a grid they can use to record words they will be reading in a text that has been divided into parts. Each group will read a specific section looking for specific words and word relationships.

6. Once all have read their portion of the text and completed their SFA grids, display the grids and discuss them as a whole group. Point out the commonalities and differences found in the grids.

7. Provide students with an SFA grid they can use to document how they use their understanding to take action in their own lives.

Classroom Voices

The cafeteria staff reports that Betsy's second graders need to learn more about appropriate manners. Betsy is confident that her students can learn these manners and designs a lesson to explicitly teach them. Her overall goal is to help students understand that different contexts require different manners. She decides to use the SFA because it will enable students to use what they know to learn more about manners. She begins her lesson by asking students to get with a friend they feel comfortable talking with, and then says, "I'd like you all to think of a time when you know that you've been *naughty*. It doesn't matter if you got caught or not, just briefly share your story about this instance with your friend."

After giving students time to share their stories with one another, Betsy directs students back to their seats on which she has placed a sticky note. She asks students to reflect on the story they just shared with a friend and to think of another word besides *naughty* that can be used to describe their behavior. She clarifies, "I'd like you to write one word on this sticky note that could complete this sentence: Someone who is naughty may be _____ (rude, annoying, obnoxious, irresponsible, mean, etc.). As soon as you write your word, place it on the line on the board at the front of the room. If you see another sticky note with the same word, place your sticky note above that one."

As students complete their sticky notes and bring them to the board, Betsy arranges all of them so that they resemble a bar graph. She reads the students' ideas aloud so that students can verify that their words are related to *naughty* and hear all displayed words.

Class-Generated SFA Grid					
Naughtiness is . . .	**A** _____	**B** _____	**C** _____	**D** _____	**E** _____
Rude					
Annoying					
Irresponsible					
Mean					

▶ Figure 4.5 *Class-Generated SFA Grid*

Betsy's Demonstration	
Naughtiness Behaviors	**Zany Zelda**
Rude	+
Annoying	+
Irresponsible	+
Mean	--

Figure 4.6 *Betsy's Demonstration*

Betsy and her students select the four most common synonyms for naughty and use them to create a semantic feature analysis grid (see Figure 4.5). Betsy calls attention to the letters across the top of the 11x14 grid as she tapes it to the board. Holding up four other blank grids, Betsy explains to students that they are going to be reading about naughty children in the book *M Is for Mischief: An A to Z of Naughty Children* (Ashman, 2008) and will determine what type of naughtiness these children are demonstrating. She uses Zany Zelda, the last character in the book, to demonstrate how to complete the grid (see Figure 4.6). She explains that each group will complete a grid and that the grids will then be combined onto the class grid.

Following Betsy's demonstration, students get in their groups of five and each silently read one assigned poem describing the naughty actions of a child. After reading their poem, students summarize it for their group members and as a group fill out their SFA grid using (+) and (-) to indicate what type of naughtiness each character portrayed.

To conclude the lesson, Betsy collects all five grids, folds over the left side column of four of them and tapes them up side by side for all students to see and discuss. Betsy uses this discussion to lead students into the taking-action activity, stating, "Now that we have studied what NOT to do, let's discuss what actions you can take to prevent such naughty behaviors from creeping into your life!"

Betsy distributes half-sheet grids, titled *Names for Nice*, explaining that nice is often used as the opposite of naughty. She continues, "We talked about names for naughty, like

Names for Nice				
Name _____				
Ways to Be Nice	Classroom	Cafeteria	Playground	Home
Polite				
Pleasant				
Responsible				
Kind				

▶ Figure 4.7 *Names for Nice*

rude and *mean*, so let's now turn our attention to names for nice. What word would you use to describe children that are the opposite of rude?" Luke raises his hand, offering *polite* as a suggestion. Once students have four related words (see Figure 4.7), Betsy comments, "Being nice is one way of showing that you have good manners. Use this grid to show where you used your manners today."

Extensions

1. Split the class into groups, with each group taking responsibility for a particular context, such as a football game, a formal restaurant, a birthday party, and so on. Have each student group consider the manners that are expected in each of these settings and create a "How To" brochure to teach others about manners in these settings.

2. Help students become more aware of the manners they do understand by having an older student group teach a younger group about manners that should be used in various school settings, such as the library, the hallways, and the cafeteria.

3. Discuss with students what they can do in situations when others are not using manners. Should they say something, or just model better behavior? As a class in a shared or interactive writing session, create a list of tips for kids on appropriate ways to handle situations such as these.

Web Sites

www.emilypost.com/kidsandparents/index.htm consists of tips, games, printables, and advice for teaching manners to children ranging from ages three through teen.

www.childdevelopmentinfo.com/parenting/manners.shtml provides advice for teaching manners in various contexts. The site also provides useful books for helping kids with manners.

www.bblocks.samhsa.gov is a site covering a wide variety of topics through games for kids, lesson plans, and advice for parents. Topics include manners, hygiene, physical fitness, and others.

Tips for Professional Collaboration

School Lunch Personnel: Suggest that lunchroom workers post a sign showing appropriate lunchroom manners. Call attention to those students who show evidence of using specific manners.

Don't Be Bullied!

Description

Social Fitness: For whatever reason, bullying is on the rise in the United States and abroad. This is troubling because, as noted by the ASCD Commission on the Whole Child (2007), for optimal learning to occur, all children need a place where they feel safe and secure. This same commission notes that while youth in all countries engage in some form of bullying, students in the United States rank among the highest for frequent bullying. Just why children feel the need to bully others is a topic that many continue to investigate. Note not only that bullying does occur but that there are different types of bullying. One of the best ways to help children combat bullying is to teach them how to recognize bullying behaviors and what to do if they suspect they are being bullied.

FitLit Suggestions

Title	Author	Publisher/Year	Suggested Grade Levels
Jay McGraw's Life Strategies for Dealing with Bullies	Jay McGraw	Aladdin/2008	4–6
Just Kidding	Trudy Ludwig	Tricycle Press/2006	K–3
Safe at Home	Sharon Robinson	Scholastic Press/2006	3–5
Sorry!	Trudy Ludwig	Tricycle Press/2006	K–2
Would I Ever Lie to You?	Caralyn Buehner	Dial Books for Young Readers/2007	K–2

Reading: Reflective discussions are vehicles for helping students develop their critical thinking skills and apply them to reading. *The Intra-Act Procedure* (Vacca and Vacca, 2008) is one way to engage students with this type of discussion. It calls for students to use the distinct but related components of comprehension, relating, valuation, and reflection during small-group discussions. Students use not only reading but the other language arts to construct and show their understanding of a given topic.

Uniting social fitness and reading, Don't Be Bullied! provides students a safe forum for discussing an ever-increasing issue for students. Using a topic of interest and concern, students use all literacy domains to come to a better understanding of bullying and what they can do about it.

Teaching Procedures

1. Explain the stages of intra-act, beginning with clear expectations for each stage of the small-group literature circle discussion. You might want to make a chart large enough for all to see or provide one for each small group.

Intra-Act Stages:

• Summarize the text. (comprehending)

Literacy Lessons to Help Kids Get Fit & Healthy

- Provide personal reactions to text ideas in summary. (relating)

- Use the game sheet to record personal reactions to statements and predictions of others' reactions. (valuing)

- Score the game sheets and discuss any reactions. (reflecting)

2. Create an intra-act game sheet such as the one shown in Figure 4.8. Write key statements down the left-hand side and designate a place for students to record how they think each individual group member will respond to each statement (agree or disagree).

3. Identify multiple copies of four texts that are all related to the same topic, in this case, bullying. Use what you know about your students to divide them into groups that are able to read the assigned text with relative ease. Most often, texts will be used for multiple days within a content unit.

4. Pose a focus question for all groups to address during and after reading.

5. Allow approximately 20 minutes for small-group discussions, facilitating as needed.

6. Bring the whole class back together to synthesize discussions and revisit the focus question.

7. Provide students with a reminder of how they can use what they know to take some action to ward off bullying.

Classroom Voices

Dave has noticed that some of his fifth-grade students' journal entries are focusing on bullying and this concerns him. He decides to meet the issue head-on by having students read about and discuss bullying. He recognizes that bullying is a complex issue and that it will take several lessons for students to fully understand it, so he plans a unit. On this third day of the unit, Dave continues using the five different books, all related to bullying, that different groups have been reading. He also continues to have students use intra-act as a way of reading and discussing their texts.

He begins by having students get into the literature discussion groups and uses the overhead transparency to review the topics students have previously discussed. He comments, "In the past couple of days, we have been learning a lot about bullying. On Monday we focused on what makes a bully. On Tuesday you read and discussed ideas for addressing bullying. Today what we are going to focus on is detecting whether you think you are being bullied." He continues by writing and reading the day's focus question on the overhead transparency, "How do you determine if someone is bullying you? Remember," he adds, "I'm not looking for you to answer this question right now. Instead, this is the question you will keep at the front of your minds as you read your texts today and participate in your small-group discussions." Dave then directs students to pick up their texts and the intra-act game sheets and gives them time to read and respond to their texts.

After about 20 minutes, the group reading *Max Quigley: Technically NOT a Bully* (Roy, 2009) is finishing up the seventh chapter of the novel. Students are rereading their marked passages and are getting ready to hear Elizabeth's summary of the chapter. She begins by saying, "Well, the first part of the chapter is talking about how Max doesn't really think he's a bully because he doesn't try to hurt people, like by punching them or anything. Then his dad and mom say that he *is* a bully and has to go to the kid's house to apologize to him." The other students in the group nod in agreement, so Elizabeth continues, "So they go to the kid's house (you know, the one he calls 'Nerdstrom'), and his mom, Mrs. Nordstrom, she cries and stuff when Max apologizes to . . . oh yea, Triffin. Well, Triffin thinks Max's apology is bogus and yells at him and all the parents for making his life even more difficult because he knows that Max is just going to keep bullying him and will probably get worse." Satisfied, Elizabeth asks the students in the group if anyone has anything else to add to the summary. A few students in the group add in a few details supporting what Elizabeth has said, which leads to the relating portion of their discussion.

The students engage in a spirited conversation, offering their opinions about how Max has treated Triffin, and about what bullying really is. Then Ernesto offers his comment, "Yea, but that kid Triffin is kinda being dumb about the whole thing. Max was joking around, and the kid's mom came and got him anyway. I bet he only sat out there at the

Intra-Act Game Sheet

Name _Elizabeth_   Text _Max Quigley: Technically NOT a Bully_

Date _4-26-09_   Pages _Ch. 7 p. 23-35_

Total Score _____   Percentage of Correct Predictions _____

Names →	Elizabeth	Mark	Ernesto	Maria
1. Bullies should be forced to apologize to their victims face-to-face.	(A) D	A (D)	A (D)	A (D)
2. It's not bullying when it's with your brother or sister.	A (D)	(A) D	(A) D	A (D)
3. Someone should only be called a bully if they're causing physical pain to someone.	A (D)	A (D)	(A) D	A (D)
4. Some kids are just too sensitive and need to learn to lighten up and take a joke. Jokes are not really bullying.	A (D)	A (D)	(A) D	A (D)
5. Victims should stand up to bullies and tell them how they feel.	(A) D	(A) D	A (D)	(A) D

▶ Figure 4.8 *Intra-Act Game Sheet*

factory for like 15 minutes. What's the big deal?" His comments prompt other students to share their thoughts, including Mark's question about apologizing: "Don't you think all the parents just made the whole thing worse than it already was? I mean, now the whole grade is probably going to know about it. And I think Triffin is right about getting mocked even more now. BIG mistake." Hearing this, Elizabeth, the group leader, decides that it's time for all of them to take out their intra-act game sheet. Elizabeth reads each statement carefully, thinks about the group's conversation, and fills out her game sheet (Figure 4.8), circling her own responses to the prompts and putting a square around her predictions for others' responses. She waits in anticipation as the rest of the group finishes up.

Noticing that all groups are finished with reading and completing their intra-act game sheets, Dave brings the whole class together. He states, "I heard a lot of interesting discussions today as I listened in on different groups." Pointing to the guiding question, Dave continues, "Remember that our guiding question was 'How do you determine if someone is bullying you?' Take some time to share your ideas with the whole class."

After about ten minutes, Dave closes the lesson by encouraging children to use what they know about bullying. He comments, "Now that you have a better understanding of bullying, you need to take action when you feel you are being bullied. You can use this bookmark as a reminder of bullying behaviors and suggestions for dealing with them."

Extensions

1. Give students a copy of the Is It Bullying? chart (Figure 4.10), and an envelope containing examples of behaviors observed on the playground, in the classroom, on the bus, and elsewhere. Tell students to read each statement carefully and then put it in the most appropriate place on their chart. After the chart is complete, students get into groups of two or three to discuss the similarities and differences they noticed in their placement of behaviors they've experienced.

Bullying Bookmark

Bullying Behaviors:
1. Targets someone who appears to be weak
2. Uses threats to get someone to do something
3. Calls people names
4. Ridicules an individual

Your Actions:
1. Ignore
2. Use assertive voice
3. Get away
4. Get help from someone

▶ Figure 4.9 *Bullying Bookmark*

Is It Bullying?		
NOT	**MAYBE**	**DEFINITELY**

▶ Figure 4.10 *Is It Bullying?*

Literacy Lessons to Help Kids Get Fit & Healthy

2. Share a bullying scenario with the students, then pass out cards to each of the students with a name of one of the persons in the scenario. Ask students to put themselves in the shoes of this person and discuss the feelings each person would experience in that scenario.

3. Help students recognize what events may lead up to a bullying situation through discussions of literature with bullying as a topic or through students' stories. Instead of bullying, how could the situation have been prevented?

Web Sites

www.pacerkidsagainstbullying.org is an interactive site designed for kids to understand what bullying is, hear and see what other kids have to say about bullying, and take a stand against bullying. Kids can cast their vote on various issues and take an oath to speak up against bullying.

www.loveourchildrenusa.org provides resources for parents, educators, and children. It includes information about advocacy groups, teaching materials, legislative information, and games for kids and teens.

www.stopcyberbullying.org describes what cyberbullying is, who engages in cyberbullying, and how parents, educators, and children can work together to address the problem.

Tips for Professional Collaboration

Media Specialist: Ask a computer expert to have children use the Internet to investigate cyber bullying. What is it? Who is most likely to engage in cyber bullying? What can a person do to take action against cyber bullying?

CHAPTER 5

Integrating
EMOTIONAL FITNESS
AND LITERACY

As with the research findings that lend support to the importance of physical and nutritional fitness to accelerate learning, so, too, is there compelling support for the impact of social and emotional fitness on optimizing children's learning (Goleman, 1995; ASCD, 2007; NASP, 2008). In sum, to best achieve in school and in life, children need to be socially fit (discussed in Chapter 4) and emotionally fit (the topic of this chapter).

Emotional fitness concerns itself with skills such as helping children understand emotions (e.g., fear, enjoyment), developing a positive outlook about themselves (self- esteem), believing in one's ability to successfully initiate and perform a given task (self-efficacy), establishing realistic goals and taking steps toward achieving them, and understanding how to effectively identify and solve problems. While some children might be naturally outfitted with emotional fitness, most are not. They need to learn these most important skills through explicit teaching. In the words of the National Association of School Psychologists (2008, p. 2), "A comprehensive 21st-century education also teaches students social-emotional competence, self-control, problem-solving, and conflict-resolution skills."

What better way to help children learn about emotional fitness than by using literacy? The two are intimately connected. Consider the many times when you have an emotional response to something you read. You may have caught yourself laughing aloud, stopping to ponder a thought that grabs your attention, or writing a comment in the margin. At other times, you may find yourself in an emotionally charged discussion when sharing your ideas with others. All of these are emotional, or *aesthetic,* responses (Rosenblatt, 2002).

Showing children how to use reading and the other language arts to enhance their emotional fitness is the focus of this chapter. Figure 5.1 is an overview of the emotional fitness activities and content literacy teaching strategies in this chapter.

	Here's looking at you! (positive self-image)	How do you feel? (emotions)	You Can Do It! (self-efficacy)	Set and Meet a Goal	Solve your Problem
Discussion Web			x		
Double-Entry Journal		x			
Idea Circle					x
Selective Reading Guide				x	
Text Annotations	x				
Alternate Perspectives					x
Evaluating Images	x				
Posing Problems					x
Juxtaposing	x	x			
Taking Action	x	x	x	x	x

▶ Figure 5.1 *Emotional Fitness Lessons and Content Reading Skills*

Here's Looking at You!

Description

Emotional Fitness: A look at toys and advertisements helps explain why many girls and boys have a less than favorable view of their bodies. For girls, trim is in and for guys it's all about having a muscular physique. Those who do not fit these standards (and that would be the majority) typically suffer with poor self-images. One of the best ways to help children combat these unrealistic images is to teach them about their unique differences and provide them with opportunities to appreciate them.

Reading: Active reading requires readers to interact with texts and the authors of texts in a variety of ways, ultimately leading to heightened critical thinking. Text annotations (Vacca and Vacca, 2008), and specifically the critical-note text annotation, inspire critical thinking while reading a text. With teacher guidance, students first examine an author's message and then form and write their own position about it. Critical-note text annotations enhance and support divergent thinking.

Combining emotional fitness and reading, in Here's Looking at You!, students use all literacy domains and critical thinking to examine and explore ideas related to body image. The overall objective is to help children see that regardless of how they are portrayed in the media, body types differ and are rarely, if ever, ideal.

FitLit Suggestions

Title	Author	Publisher/Year	Suggested Grade Levels
Girls Hold Up This World	Jada Pinkett-Smith	Scholastic Inc./2005	K–3
Jalapeño Bagels	Natasha Wing	Atheneum Books for Young Readers/1996	1–3
My People	Langston Hughes	Atheneum Books for Young Readers/2009	K–5
Oddly	Joyce Dunbar	Candlewick Press/2009	K–2
Tough Chicks	Cece Meng	Clarion Books/2009	K–2

Teaching Procedures

1. Form a critical-thinking question related to the topic students will be reading to guide the lesson and display it for all to see. For example, when exploring body image, you

Literacy Lessons to Help Kids Get Fit & Healthy

might ask, "How do manufacturers portray images through toys?"

2. Demonstrate how to complete a critical-note text annotation by using one page or section of a text that conveys the author's message. *The Best Part of Me* (Ewald, 2002) is one example.

3. Divide the text so that one pair of students can read and create a critical note for the section they will read.

4. Bring the whole group together to discuss how to use critical-note text annotations to answer the guiding question. Record this information on a chart and keep it visible throughout the lesson. Students will complete it to conclude the lesson.

5. After students have read the first text and completed a critical-note text annotation for it, select another text and have the students repeat the process.

6. Once both texts have been read and students have created their annotations, visually juxtapose the two critical annotations in a two-column chart. Doing so will heighten the level of critical thinking students will use to answer the guiding question of the lesson.

7. Engage students in a whole-group discussion about the juxtaposed texts and the guiding question.

8. Close the lesson with the taking-action activity so that students can apply the ideas in their own lives.

Classroom Voices

Reflecting on years past, Mary recalls that she can expect her current fifth-grade students' preoccupation with body image, especially toward the end of the year when students' anxiety over the transition to middle school is all the buzz. Despite the heartache Mary feels watching students grow increasingly uncomfortable in their own skin, she knows that they need to both recognize and manage their emotions about how they look. Still, she wonders how she can ease their minds and help them put their concerns about body image into perspective.

She designs a lesson that begins with a text written by elementary students, *The Best Part of Me* (Ewald, 2002). She begins the lesson with the whole group, stating, "In every text we read, the author strives to convey messages to readers. At times, these messages are literally stated, they are 'right there.' At other times we need to seek them out, looking beneath the words and/or pictures on the page. We need to 'think and search.'" Displaying the book, she continues, "Wendy Ewald created this book with many messages from children just like you. Today, we will start by determining these messages. Let's start with a guiding question. I'll write it on the board for you to see." She writes, 'What message is the author conveying with the character development in this text?'

In order to facilitate responses to this question, Mary uses the first page of *The Best Part of Me* (Ewald, 2002) to briefly review the text annotations strategy that students have been learning, commenting, "You already know how to read a part of a text and how to make some notes about it. Today I want you to use what you know to make a new kind of annotation. It's called critical note annotation." She demonstrates the critical note by first reading aloud and then using the following sentences written on a mock index card displayed on the board:

"Eyes are important not only for seeing, but because they tell a lot too. People show emotions, such as sadness and anger, with their eyes. Everyone's eyes are unique and we should pay attention to what they communicate."

Mary points out two aspects of the note she'd like students to remember when using this strategy with their assigned text page in the next part of the lesson. "First," Mary points out, "remember that you need to show the author's message, then you need to share your own position on that message." Once students have had time to ask questions and understand how to complete the critical text annotation, Mary gives them time to pair up and provides each a copy of the text to read. She then observes as each pair reads a page, studies the photograph, and records their critical note on an index card.

Once all student pairs have completed their tasks, she calls the whole group together. In turn, she has each pair read aloud their page and their critical notes for each page. Mary

Body Images in Texts	
Wendy Ewald	**Disney**

Figure 5.2 *Body Images in Texts*

poses the guiding question once again, and creates a two-column chart (see Figure 5.2) for students to record responses so that all can see. They will complete the left side of the chart today. In the second part of the lesson, which will be completed in the computer lab on the following day, students will continue to use this chart by completing the right side and juxtaposing the two columns.

The following day, Mary reviews the two-column chart and instructs students in the next portion of the lesson. She begins by asking students to name their favorite television shows. She writes each title on an index card and displays them in the pocket chart. Mary then breaks students into groups of three to investigate character development in one of their favorites, Disney. She instructs students to look at a different Disney show shown on the Disney Channel or Web site.

Once again, Mary passes out an index card to each student group, and directs students to write the name of their show and to create a critical note regarding the producers' message and then their own position on the message, stating, "Remember that you're studying the characters in these shows, looking for similarities, differences, what you hear them say, and so on, to identify what you think the producer of the show is communicating to you, the audience. Then discuss this with your group and determine what your position is on this message." Students quickly set to work clicking through the site, conversing with one another, and even displaying a bit of surprise as they consider what to record on their critical note.

After reviewing and discussing each of the critical notes with the whole group, the students return their attention to the two-column chart (Figure 5.2) and are full of ideas regarding the Disney producers' messages. Without prompting them, Mary notices that students compare the two columns, juxtaposing the authors' messages. This is just the level of critical thinking Mary was hoping to instill. Mary concludes the lesson stating, "So as you can see, different authors and creators of television shows have many different ideas about how a body should look. You have also had time to form some of your own ideas. You can now use what you know to create your own "Best Part of Me" page for a class slide show. You'll need to use your technology skills to complete this page. Once all are finished, we'll decide whether you want to have them displayed for parent-teacher conference night next week."

Extensions

1. As a math activity in ratios and measurement, ask students to measure a popular doll and then to use ratios to compare these measurements to those of real humans. Discuss the implications of the unrealistic nature of the dolls' bodies.

2. Ask students to apply their critical-thinking skills to watching TV for homework! Assign a treasure hunt for messages about body image portrayed to them through TV shows, advertisements, and movies they're watching on TV. Challenge students to find similarities and differences between characters created for TV and the real people in their lives.

3. Invite students to create a TV show that could more accurately demonstrate lives of kids their age. Encourage students to think about the characters in the show and what messages they'd want to send to viewers through these characters.

Web Sites

www.bam.gov and *www.bodyimagehealth.org* are sites designed for kids addressing body and mind through critical-thinking activities and information focused on nutrition, safety, physical activity, and the stresses, conflicts, and other realities of kids' lives.

www.healthyweight.net presents information to improve adult awareness of research on obesity, eating disorders, dieting, and guidelines for healthy living at any size. The site includes specific links to information applicable to children.

Tips for Professional Collaboration

School Counselor: Enlist the help of the school counselor in acquiring resources such as articles and Web sites that will help elicit conversations about this topic with parents of those children struggling with poor self-image.

How Do You Feel?

Description

Emotional Fitness: Goleman (1995, p. 289) defines emotion as a "feeling and its distinctive thoughts." He proposes that there are numerous emotions, each with variations. Anger, sadness, fear, enjoyment, and love are among the emotions individuals experience. Emotional fitness entails becoming aware of such emotions and how to appropriately manage them. Awareness and management are teaching points that enable children to better understand the emotional sides of themselves. The goal is to help children understand that having a range of emotions is natural and acceptable. Managing them well is something most students need to learn.

Reading: One of the best ways for children to explore their thoughts about reading is through writing. Double-entry journal (Vacca and Vacca, 2008) is one of the many ways to use writing to crack open reading. Just as the name implies, learners use writing to juxtapose their ideas and feelings relative to a given prompt, causing them to think critically about what others have to say and feel noting similarities and differences among their ideas and feelings.

FitLit Suggestions

Title	Author	Publisher/Year	Suggested Grade Levels
The Feelings Book	Todd Parr	Megan Tingley Books/2001	K–2
Feelings to Share from A to Z	Todd Snow	Maren Green Publishing/2007	K–3
Game Day	Tiki & Ronde Barber	Simon & Schuster Books for Young Readers/2005	3–4
I Miss You Every Day	Simms Taback	Viking/2007	K–2
What Does Peace Feel Like?	V. Radunky	Atheneum Books for Young Readers/2004	K–5

Connecting emotional fitness and reading, How Do You Feel? enables learners to use a critical literacy skill (juxtaposing) to sharpen their understanding of emotions. They also learn how they can identify and act on their emotions in acceptable ways.

Teaching Procedures

1. Bring the whole class together to brainstorm a list of words used to identify feelings. Write these feeling words on a chart to remain visible throughout the lesson.

2. Explain how these words are likely to turn up in the book *Shy Guy* (Tibo, 2002), then read the text aloud, stopping occasionally for comprehension checks and to connect the text to the chart of feeling words when appropriate.

3. Ask the students to partner-share a retelling of the book, focusing on beginning, middle, and end. Think about what is different about the beginning of the book compared to the end.

4. Give students the double-entry journal form, explain the directions for using it, provide time for individual students to complete it, and then have students pair up with a friend to share their responses.

5. Close the lesson with a brief discussion of how we may feel very differently about things than our friends do, and why it's important to learn and practice positive ways of sharing our emotions with our friends. This leads to the "taking action" portion of the lesson.

Classroom Voices

Kim's second-grade classroom community is really coming together. The students have established routines, and have worked hard to learn the types of social skills that make the community learn and play together with rarely a hitch. Yet, a few of her students remain aloof, almost painfully shy. Although these students are new to the school, Kim still feels as if their emotions are holding them back from participating in collaborative learning, and building friendships in the class. Kim has observed other students in the class attempting to get them involved, but with little success.

Understanding the value of connections with characters in literature, Kim decides to address some of the students' emotional difficulties by reading the book *Shy Guy* (Tibo, 2002) and having students use double-entry journal responses to bring to the fore some of the feelings expressed by the main character, which are similar to those of her students. Kim begins her lesson with the whole group gathered on the carpet. Marker in hand, Kim begins, "I'd like you to think back through all the events of your day so far, starting from the moment you woke up this morning. Pick one event and think about how you were feeling at that moment. Briefly share your idea with the friend sitting next to you." After students take two minutes to share the event, Kim asks, "Now, I'd like to fill this entire chart with all the feeling words that I heard you using as you told your story. Let's go around the circle and say your feeling out loud while I write it on this chart so that you all can see."

After the chart is full of all the feeling words, Kim introduces the read-aloud text. "In this text, you'll meet a boy that feels many of these same emotions that you've all felt. As I read, listen to see if the author uses some of your feeling words." Kim reads through *Shy Guy*, pausing for comprehension checks and students' connections to the feeling words chart. At the completion of the read-aloud, Kim asks the students to practice their retelling

Double-entry Journal	
In the story	**In your mind**
"I was shy. I had trouble with words. They got stuck in my throat. When I tried to talk, I choked up and blushed."	
"I'm hardly shy at all anymore. I talk to everyone, and everyone talks to me. My friends come to play at my house , , ,"	

▶ Figure 5.3 *Double-entry Journal*

skills by sitting knee-to-knee and taking turns retelling the story from beginning to end.

Following the retelling practice, Kim hands out the double-entry journal page (see Figure 5.3), and explains what she would like students to do. "After you've read the beginning of this story again in the first box, explain on the right side how you felt about it. Then do this again for the ending of the story." After individual students finish completing their writing, Kim instructs students to pair up with a friend and share their responses.

To bring closure to the lesson, Kim brings the students together and asks, "First, how did the beginning of the book compare to the end of the book? Were the feelings the same, or different?" and then, "So did your friends feel the same way you did about the parts of the book?" Kim facilitates the brief discussion and then transitions the students into the taking-action portion of the lesson, another opportunity to use the double-entry journal.

Taking-Action Form	
I feel . . .	**I express this by . . .**
enjoyment	
sadness	
anger	
fear	
love	

▶ Figure 5.4 *Taking-Action Form*

Literacy Lessons to Help Kids Get Fit & Healthy

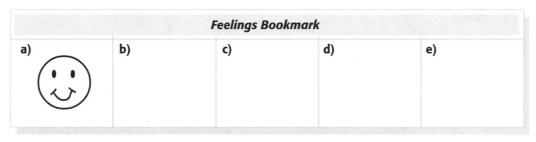

Feelings Bookmark				
a)	b)	c)	d)	e)

▶ Figure 5.5 *Feelings Bookmark*

She explains how sometimes friends' feelings are very different from each other, and that it can cause some problems in their friendship when these are misunderstood. "This is why it's important to understand positive ways to express the emotions we feel. This will help our relationships with each other and our classroom community." Kim then models how to complete the taking-action form (see Figure 5.4) with a few examples from her own life.

Extensions

1. Divide the class into mixed groups of five, and give a bookmark (see Figure 5.5) to each student in each group. Give each group one brief scenario written on an index card. One group member volunteers to read aloud the scenario to the group, then all draw a face in the corresponding box on the bookmark that would show their feelings in response to that situation in their own lives. Students are prompted to briefly discuss with others in the group the face they drew, and why they'd feel that way. They then pass that index card scenario to the next group in the room. Repeat steps 1–4 until all cards have been passed.

2. Use the bookmark to have students track the emotions of a main character in any read-aloud. Stop at intervals in the story and have students either draw the emotion or write the feeling word in the box.

3. Play charades with the feelings words, having students take turns acting out a feeling word, while others attempt to guess by reading the nonverbal cues of the actor/actress.

Web Sites

www.pbskids.org/arthur/games/aboutface/aboutface.html is a site designed for students in grades 1–3 in which students listen to a story and then indicate what the character is feeling in each part of the story by clicking on the face that shows the correct emotion.

www.cyh.com/SubDefault.aspx?p=255 incorporates kids' artwork in friendly language addressing "everything to do with being a kid." The site includes information about health-related topics, such as "Your Body," "Your Safety," and "Your Feelings."

www.kidsmatter.edu.au provides educators with assistance in creating a positive school community and tips to enhance the social and emotional learning for students in the classroom community.

Tips for Professional Collaboration

School Counselor: Have the school counselor revisit the concept of different feelings for the same situation depending on the perspectives of those in the situation. Have students role-play incidents you observe on the playground, asking students in the audience to describe the feelings experienced by each person within the incident.

You Can Do It!

Description

Emotional Fitness: Self-efficacy, a person's perceived ability and confidence to complete a given task, is another dimension of emotional fitness (Bandura, 1997). Learners are more inclined to approach any given activity if they inwardly feel that they can meet success with it and are therefore willing to risk trying. As a result of trial and error, students begin to develop ideas about themselves relative to given activities. If they are successful, they are more likely to see themselves as capable relative to that particular activity. The reverse is

FitLit Suggestions

Title	Author	Publisher/Year	Suggested Grade Levels
The Big Cheese of Third Street	Laurie H. Anderson	Simon & Schuster Books for Young Readers/2002	K–2
Keisha Ann Can!	Daniel Kirk	G.P. Putnam's Sons/2008	K
Luke Goes to Bat	Rachel Isadora	G.P. Putnam's Sons/2005	K–2
Mighty Jackie: The Strike-Out Queen	Marissa Moss	Simon & Schuster Books for Young Readers/2004	3–4
You Can Do It!	Tony Dungy	Little Simon Inspirations/2008	2–3

also true. Often, these self-perceptions have a lasting effect. How many times, for example, have you heard an adult say, "I'm not very good at . . ." (you fill in the words)?

Fortunately, self-efficacy is not static. Recognizing that students might be feeling uneasy about a new activity, teachers can actually set up students for success by designing lessons that gradually shift more of the learning onto students' shoulders. The result is that students are left with an "I can do that!" attitude and therefore are open to taking risks. Past experiences have helped them see that they are more often successful than not. Because of this confidence, they also see that their performance does not always have to be perfect.

Reading: Emotions often kick into high gear when students are engaged in thoughtful discussions. The discussion web (Alverman, 1991) is one way to facilitate these thoughtful discussions. In addition to stating what they consider to be important points, students listen to one another's ideas and consider whether they agree or disagree and state why. They then use writing to take a final stand based on all they have read and discussed.

Uniting emotional fitness and reading, You Can Do It! provides a forum for students to read, discuss, and form their own ideas. As a result of participating in a supportive discussion, students learn more about emotional fitness (self-efficacy) by first discussing it and then using reading and writing to record their ideas. They leave the lesson with an "I can" attitude about their ability to use literacy to better understand themselves.

Teaching Procedures (based on Alverman, 1991)

1. Prepare students for reading by activating their background knowledge, raising questions, making predictions, and setting a purpose for reading.

2. Assign the text and provide time for students to read it.

3. After reading, introduce a discussion web (see Figure 5.6) with a question related to the text they have just read.

4. Pair students and provide them with some time to discuss and provide reasons for why they might answer "Yes" and "No."

5. Form a group of four by putting two partner groups together. Have each compare their responses and come to a group consensus that shows their overall thinking about the question. Emphasize to students that they can disagree with one another but that in the end, they need to agree on a conclusion.

6. Have each group select a spokesperson to report out on their best possible conclusion.

7. Once each group has shared, provide time for the class to discuss ideas.

8. Have students show individual accountability by writing their own response to the discussion web question. (This is an optional follow-up activity.)

Classroom Voices

It is the start of a new school year and Jill wants her second graders to begin it with an "I can" attitude. She decides to use *The OK Book* (Rosenthal, 2007) because it helps students to see that learning is about being willing to be OK at several activities. After preparing students for reading by having students make some predictions about the book, Jill had the students read the book in small groups yesterday. Today she is going to take the lesson a

Literacy Lessons to Help Kids Get Fit & Healthy

step further by posing a question related to the book and giving students time to arrive at their own conclusions. She calls the whole group together and once they are settled begins by holding up a copy of *The OK Book* and stating, "Yesterday you had some time to read this book but little time to discuss it. That's what we are going to do today. We're going to use the discussion web."

She proceeds by referring students to the discussion web (see Figure 5.6), commenting, "You will notice that there is a question in the middle and a place for you to indicate your reasons for whether you agree or disagree. You and your partner are going to talk about the question and write your reasons for agreeing or disagreeing. Let's give it a try." Jill has students meet with their previously assigned partners, gives them a copy of the discussion web, and provides time for them to discuss it. After a few minutes, she states, "It looks to me like all partners have had some time to discuss the question and to come up with some reasons for their answers. Now I need two partner groups to join so that we have small groups of four. Go ahead and get yourselves arranged." After students have had some time to relocate and situate themselves, Jill provides the next set of directions. "Your job this time is to discuss your ideas with one another. You might not all agree and that's perfectly acceptable. But what you will need to do after you have discussed is to agree on a conclusion. Choose a recorder to write the conclusion in the space shown on the form. You will then choose a reporter to report out to the whole class."

	Discussion Web for The OK Book	
No	**Is being OK better than being perfect?**	**Yes**
	Conclusion	

▶ Figure 5.6 *Discussion Web for* The OK Book

I Can and I'm OK		
Name		
Day	**I can**	**Here's how I know I'm OK:**

▶ Figure 5.7 I Can and I'm OK

Jill provides time for students to talk, dropping in on groups as necessary. She wants to make sure that all students get to participate and that all feel OK about the group's conclusion. Once she sees that all groups have arrived at a conclusion, she reconvenes the whole class and provides time for the reporter from each group to share. Eric leads stating, "Our group came up with the conclusion that there's really no such thing as being perfect. It seems like there is always a way to be better." Michele adds, "That's what we decided. Like even though you can read, you still might have some troubles and that's OK. You don't have to read perfect. You just have to understand." Jamie chimes in, "Well, some in our group said you do have to be perfect sometimes and sometimes that it's OK to be not so perfect." Jill probes, "Tell us more." "Well," Jamie adds, "it's like when you are trying to find an answer to a math problem. You have to find the perfect answer. But other times, like when you are playing baseball, you might be OK, but not perfect. I mean, you might not get a hit every time. You might strike out. It's OK, though, because you are having fun playing the game and you still feel OK."

Picking up on Jamie's comment, Jill states, "It sounds to me like all of you have come to agree that being OK at a lot of things is fine. You do not have to be perfect at anything. When you let go of the idea of being perfect, you free yourself up to try a lot of new activities. You realize that nobody is perfect and that learning takes some risks. That's exactly what you are going to do the rest of this year in second grade. You are going to try a lot of different things that will be new to you and the fun will be in the learning. Part of being healthy is paying attention to what you can do. In fact, I'm going to give each of you an 'I Can and I'm OK' chart (see Figure 5.7). You can keep a list of all the things you can do."

Extensions

1. Take pictures of children as they are completing various activities. Give children their pictures and have them write what the picture is showing. Bring students together to share their pictures. Once all have shared, display the pictures with a heading such as "Look What We Can Do!"

2. Using *The OK Book* as a pattern, invite students to make their own OK books by thinking of many different things they are OK at doing. Students can then read their books to one another.

3. Invite children to be on the lookout for activities their classmates can do. Provide a time during the day for children to share their insights with the class. Consider having students use a sentence frame such as "I noticed (name of student) trying hard to (name of activity)." Encouragement like this is one of the best ways to build self-efficacy.

Web Sites

www.powertolearn.com/games/index.shtml offers a collection of computer-based games that children can use to increase self-efficacy by challenging themselves at the appropriate level.

www.pecentral.com/lessonideas/ViewLesson.asp?ID-8722 is a poetry writing lesson titled "I Am Special" aimed at helping intermediate-grade children understand and appreciate what they can do by creating an "I Am" poem.

Tips for Professional Collaboration

Physical Educator: Ask the physical education instructor to challenge children to try out a new game and point out how well they performed. Emphasize the importance of being willing to take a risk at trying something new rather than being afraid of being less than perfect.

Set and Meet a Goal

Description

Emotional Fitness: The ability to set and achieve goals is one characteristic of an emotionally fit person (Goleman, 1995). To be most effective, though, goals need to be specific, attainable, and time-sensitive. Teaching students all three parts leads them to set realistic goals they can meet. The result is an increase in both self-esteem and self-efficacy.

Reading: While there are many types of reading guides (Wood, Lapp, Flood, and Taylor, 2008), the selective reading guide (Cunningham and Shablak, 1975) helps students glean important information from expository text. It also indirectly shows students how to adjust reading rate to their purpose for reading.

Using a selective reading guide requires some forethought. Teachers need to think through the text students will be reading and make some decisions about what it is they want students to take away from the reading experience. They should also take into consideration their students' background knowledge for the topic at hand. They then construct a guide for students to use when reading and demonstrate how to use it. Once students understand how to use the guide, the teacher shifts more of the learning onto students' shoulders by having them use it independently.

Blending emotional fitness and reading, Set and Meet a Goal helps students use literacy to establish goals. As a result of reading and analyzing how to set and achieve goals, they take action by identifying a realistic goal and establish a time line for meeting it.

FitLit Suggestions

Title	Author	Publisher/Year	Suggested Grade Levels
Becoming Joe DiMaggio	Maria Testa	Candlewick Press/2002	2–3
How Oliver Olson Changed the World	Claudia Mills	Farrar Straus Giroux/2009	2–3
I Get So Hungry	Bebe Moore Campbell	G.P. Putnam's Sons/2008	1–3
The Longest Season: The Story of the of the Orioles' 1988 Losing Streak	Cal Ripken Jr.	Philomel Books/2007	3–5
Wonder Goal!	Michael Foreman	Farrar, Straus, and Giroux/2002	1–3

Teaching Procedures

1. Read the text students will be reading and ask yourself these questions: "What is it that students need to know when they are finished reading this text? What background information do students need in order to understand the ideas that I want them to learn from this chapter?"

2. While reading, identify the information you want students to acquire.

3. Select only those sections for students to read that will enable them to acquire the information you have identified as being essential.

4. Construct a guide that directs students to the parts they need to read. See Figure 5.8 for an example.

5. Explain the purpose for the reading guide and demonstrate how to use it. Once they show an understanding of how to use the guide, have them use it independently.

6. Invite students to discuss their findings, using their guides and information they have gleaned.

Classroom Voices

Two months into the school year, Eric continues to teach his fourth graders about setting goals. His observations have led him to see that students have a pretty good grasp on establishing goals but they need a little work on understanding how to fine-tune their goals to make them more manageable and attainable. Eric has also been encouraging his students to adjust their reading rate to their purpose for reading. To that end, he has been teaching students how to skim to locate specific information.

Eric selects *Strong Man: The Story of Charles Atlas* (McCarthy, 2007) for students' reading because they will learn how a famous individual set and met goals and inspired others to do the same. Eric is ready to demonstrate how to use a selective reading guide. First, he generates interest in the text by giving students some time to talk about what they already know about setting goals. "You have been learning that one way to feel better about yourself is to set and meet goals. Let's brainstorm your ideas." Without too much hesitation, Alice blurts, "They have to be something you can really accomplish. Like I might wish for ten sisters but there is nothing I can do to make that happen." BJ adds, "You have to set a start and end time for meeting your goal." His comment invites Dustin to add, "Oh yeah! And you have to think about what you are going to do to make it happen, kind of like the steps you are going to take." As students share their ideas, Eric writes them on the board. He comments, "I am very impressed! You appear to have learned a lot about setting goals. One of the hardest things to understand about goal-setting is to make the goals easy enough to reach in a set amount of time. This is important because accomplishing a goal enables a person to experience feelings of success. Feeling successful is one way to feel better about yourself. Feeling successful also makes you want to set new goals and to stretch yourself a little further. Let's see how a famous person set goals for himself." Eric holds up the book for all to see.

He continues, "You have been working on understanding how to adjust your reading rate to your purpose for reading. Sometimes, though, the authors provide so much information that we can have a hard time finding what it is we want to know. That's where a reading guide and your teacher come in handy! Take this book, for example. I have

Literacy Lessons to Help Kids Get Fit & Healthy

Selective Reading Guide for **Strong Man: The Story of Charles Atlas**	
Name _____	Date _____
Reading Directions/Questions	**Your Ideas**
1. Read page 6. Who helped Angelo set a goal of becoming stronger? Why was being stronger important to him?	
2. Pages 9 and 10: Look at the illustrations and the text above them. What do they tell you about setting goals? What information is left out that you need to know in order to achieve your goals?	
3. Page 11: Read to discover how Angelo got the name Charles Atlas. Was it a goal of his to be so named or did others impose it onto him?	
4. Pages 21, 22: Identify three ways that Charles Atlas helped others set and meet their fitness goals.	
5. Pages 28–29: Take a look at any one exercise. Set a goal for integrating it into your daily physical activities.	

▶ Figure 5.8 *Selective Reading Guide for* Strong Man: The Story of Charles Atlas

already read it thinking about you as readers and what it is I think you should know. I then designed this guide to help you focus on the information that I want you to pay attention to when you are reading. Once you have used the guide, we'll discuss what you have discovered. I think you'll see that this guide will help you to comprehend the story, yet it will also help you read the material more quickly. Let me show you how it works."

Eric then displays the reading guide for *Strong Man: The Story of Charles Atlas* on an overhead transparency and demonstrates how to use it by reading the first few pages aloud and completing the first section (see Figure 5.8). Next, he invites students to participate by having them listen to the next part of the text as identified on the guide and having them share what they discovered. Once he sees that students understand how to use the guide, he closes the lesson saying, "It looks like you understand how to use this guide when listening to me read. You are going to do the same thing when you continue reading this book today."

Taking Action to Set a Goal		
_____'s Goal-Setting Card		
My Goal/Why I want to achieve it	My Action Plan for achieving my goal	My Time line (when I expect to start and achieve my goal)

▶ Figure 5.9 *Taking Action to Set a Goal*

Once all students have read the book and completed the guide, Eric provides time for students to discuss their findings with one another. He then reconvenes the class and states, "So now you know about how someone else set and met goals. You also discovered how much of an impact a person can have on others. Now is your chance to use what you know to establish your own goals." Eric shows students the Taking Action to Set a Goal card (Figure 5.9) and provides time for each student to write on it. "Remember," he comments, "your goal is something that is important to you."

Extensions

1. Although goals tend to be an individual matter, consider having the class set a group goal as a way of building community. For instance, students might determine how to create a litter-free school or classroom environment.

2. Have students think about alternatives to reach a goal should their first plan fail. Invite students to write out their alternative plans.

3. Provide children with some hypothetical goals (e.g., stopping bullying on school grounds, making new students feel included) and have them discuss an action plan and timeline for reaching the goals.

Web Sites

www.lessonplanet.com provides several goal-setting lessons for various grade levels.

www.literacymatters.org/content/study/organizers.htm offers many different graphic organizers to help children navigate texts.

Tips for Professional Collaboration

Physical Educator: Work with the physical education teacher to invite students to set a goal to attain some physical activity or achieve sportsmanlike conduct.

Solve Your Problem!

Description

Emotional Fitness: Different people and their accompanying opinions and ideas are sure to lead to conflicts. In fact, conflicts are natural, whereas learning how to manage them is not. One aspect of emotional fitness is learning how to do just that. It entails being able to identify a problem and what to do to resolve it as harmoniously as possible. Teaching children how to understand conflicts and healthy ways to deal with them (problem-solving) is well worth the effort if we seek to create a caring, collaborative, and harmonious community.

Reading: When children become emotionally charged about texts that matter to them, they may get into heated debates. When this occurs, students need to know how to work through the discussion and come to common understandings. Idea circles (Guthrie and McCann, 1996) provide a roundtable for this kind of discussion. Students read related but different texts all related to a common topic and discuss their findings with one another.

FitLit Suggestions

Title	Author	Publisher/Year	Suggested Grade Levels
Harriet's Had Enough	Elissa Haden Guest	Candlewick Press/2009	K–2
Louder, Lili	Gennifer Choldenko	G.P. Putnam's Sons/2007	K–2
No Dessert Forever	George Ella Lyon; Peter Catalanotto	Atheneum Books for Young Readers/2006	K–2
Sam Is Not a Loser	Thierry Robberecht	Clarion Books/2006	K–1
Stealing Home: Jackie Robinson, Against the Odds	Robert Burleigh	Simon & Schuster Books for Young Readers /2007	3–5

Combining emotional fitness and reading, Solve Your Problem! provides an authentic context for children to use language to discuss and solve problems relative to the texts they read. Students need to show that they can listen to others' ideas, looking for similarities and differences among their different texts. Disagreements are likely to occur, as are amicable solutions.

Teaching Procedures

1. Decide how many students you will engage at any one time. You might want to start by using idea circles with one group or different groups within the whole class simultaneously.

2. Identify a topic of study that is of interest to students. Students should already know something about the topic. The purpose of the idea circle is to extend their understanding.

3. Establish goals about what each group is to accomplish. They might need to create a chart showing their understandings or key ideas about their discussion or some other artifact.

4. Provide students with a variety of texts related to the topic.

5. Provide time for students to read and discuss their ideas with one another. Make sure that students know how they are to function in their groups. I usually give groups a discussion etiquette poster (see Figure 5.10).

6. Bring the class together and have each group present their major ideas.

Discussion Etiquette Poster

Discussion Etiquette

1. Focus on discussion as evidenced by body posture and eye contact.
2. Active participation (e.g., responding to ideas, sharing when appropriate).
3. Ask questions for clarification as needed.
4. Piggyback off others' ideas and thoughts.
5. Disagree constructively.
6. Listen actively.
7. Take turns letting others speak.
8. Support opinions with evidence.
9. Encourage others.

▶ Figure 5.10 *Discussion Etiquette Poster*

Classroom Voices

Shelly's fifth graders have been learning about conflict resolution for several weeks. Shelly has been focusing her instruction on identifying what causes a conflict to occur and the different ways to resolve it—to solve the problem. In this lesson, she wants students to see that conflicts and their resulting solutions can have a lasting impact for the good of all. Rather than steer clear of conflicts, then, she wants her students to expect them and learn how best to handle them. She decides to use the book *Paths to Peace: People Who Have Changed the World* (Zalben, 2006) because the content matches her objective, but also because of the format. She will be able to use idea circles by having students read and discuss the different individuals the author of the text features. Because her students are familiar with idea circles, she will do this lesson with the whole class.

She begins the lesson by reviewing with students what they have learned about identifying and solving problems in peaceful ways. She then comments, "Today we're going to take your understandings a step further. This author (she holds up the book for all to see) presents many famous individuals who had or continue to have their own ideas about

Identifying and Solving a Problem		
Name of Famous Individual _____ **My Name** _____		
What did this person see as the problem?	What did this person do to solve the problem?	What might you do to solve this problem?

▶ Figure 5.11 *Identifying and Solving a Problem*

how to help all individuals treat others humanely. The problem is their ideas were or are in conflict with others. Rather than give up, though, each figures out a way to resolve their conflicts in peaceful ways. You are going to be reading about these individuals." Shelly then has each student draw a name out of a hat. Each name corresponds to one of the individuals in the text. Once all students have a name, Shelly explains their tasks. "Each of you will read silently, looking for the information shown here." She shows the form (see Figure 5.11). Once you have identified your information, you will form a group with three other people to share your discoveries. You will also discuss how you would handle the situation. You might disagree with one another and that is acceptable. Remember that there is more than one way to solve a problem. Just remember to use what you know about discussion etiquette." After checking to make sure that all understand what they are to do, Shelly provides students with the necessary materials and provides time for them to read and respond as individuals and as a group.

Shelly closes the lesson stating, "In sitting in on different discussions, it sounds to me as if you were all able to practice what you know about identifying conflicts and solving them. Your ideas are too good to leave in your small groups, so tomorrow I am going to ask that all groups share. We'll then have some time to talk about how all individuals you read about are alike and different in terms of how they identified conflicts and what they did to solve them."

Literacy Lessons to Help Kids Get Fit & Healthy

Extensions

1. Provide students with scenarios that show conflicts and provide time for them to discuss how they would resolve the problem. Obtain four such scenarios by going to *www.KidsHealth.org/classroom/3to5/personal/growing/conflict_resolution_handout2.pdf*

2. Invite children to construct a poster that shows how to solve problems in a peaceful way. Suggest that they display their posters in the classroom, school hallways, or both.

3. Many children spend countless hours watching television. Ask them to identify their favorite show and to watch it, looking for problems that surface during an episode and how the characters resolve it. Provide time for them to share their homework findings the following day.

Web Sites

www.urbanext.uiuc.edu/conflict/index.html takes you to a conflict-resolution program titled *Out on a Limb: A Guide for Getting Along*. Aimed at third-grade students, the site offers a child-accessible explanation of three different ways to resolve problems: loud choice, soft choice, or think-and-share choice.

www.arts.gov/pub/ArtinPeacemaking.pdf is full of ideas for how to use the arts to help children solve problems, both individually and in groups.

Tips for Professional Collaboration

Media Specialist: Invite the media specialist to provide time for children to visit the *Out on a Limb: A Guide for Getting Along* program. After listening to the three different ways to resolve a problem, have children role-play each to show their understanding.

Closing Thoughts

Children need our help to become fit, and I remain optimistic that we can—with relative ease—make a big difference for them. As I noted in the Introduction, achieving wellness is a complex matter. Fortunately, there are many organizations, such as those I cite in this book, that are stepping up and doing their part to help children achieve optimal wellness. And speaking for my fellow educators, I am convinced that each one of us can do the same. Given the current state of affairs, we have little choice if we truly want children to read well to be fit and live long and healthy lives rich with promise and possibility.

References

Professional Titles

Aerobics and Fitness Association of America (AFFA). (2003). *A guide to personal fitness training*. Sherman Oaks, CA: AFFA.

Alverman, D. E. (1991). The discussion web: A graphic aid for learning across the curriculum. *The Reading Teacher, 45*: 92–99.

Anderson, S., & Whitaker, R. C. (2009). Prevalence of obesity among U.S. preschool children in different racial and ethnic groups. *Archives of Pediatrics and Adolescent Medicine, 163*: 344–348.

Armstrong, T. (1994). *Multiple intelligences in the classroom*. Alexandria, VA: Association for Supervision and Curriculum Development.

Association for Supervision and Curriculum Development. (2007). The whole child. *Infobrief, 51*: 11.

Baldwin, L. E. (1982). The relationship between physical fitness and reading comprehension scores of sixth graders. Ph.D. dis., Brigham Young University, Salt Lake City, UT.

Bandura, A. (1997). *Self-efficacy: The exercise of control*. New York: W. H. Freeman.

Barnes J. (2007). *Cross curricular learning 3–14*. London: Chapman.

Beck, I. L., McKeown, M. G., Hamilton, R. L., & Kucan, L. (1997). *Questioning the author: An approach for enhancing student engagement with text*. Newark, DE: International Reading Association.

Bennett, J. & Hanneleen. (2003). Physical education and academic performance. *Teaching Elementary Physical Education, 14* (6): 27–30.

Biernacki, M. (1993). The relationship between physical fitness development and achievement scores in mathematics and reading. Ph.D. dis., University of Southern Mississippi, Hattiesburg, MS.

Blachowicz, C., & Fisher, P. (2006). *Teaching vocabulary in all classrooms (3rd ed.)*. Upper Saddle River, NJ: Pearson.

Buell, C., & Whittaker, A. (2001). Enhancing content literacy in physical education. *Journal of Physical Education, Recreation, and Dance, 72* (6): 32–39.

Byrne, E., & Nitzke, S. (2000). Nutrition messages in a sample of children's picture books. *Journal of the American Dietetic Association, 100* (3): 359–362.

Castelli, D. M., Hillman, C. H., Buck, S. M., & Erwin, H. E. (2007). Physical fitness and academic achievement in third- and fifth-grade students. *Journal of Sport & Exercise Psychology, 29*: 239–252.

Cone, S., & Cone, T. (2001). Language arts and physical education: A natural connection. *Teaching Elementary Physical Education, 12* (4): 14–17.

Cunningham, D., & Shablak, S. L. (1975) Selective reading guide-o-rama: The content teacher's best friend. *Journal of Reading, 18*: 380–82.

Dale, D., C. Corbin, & Dale, K. (2000). Restricting opportunities to be active during school time: Do children compensate by increasing physical activity levels after school? *Research Quarterly for Exercise and Sport, 71* (3): 240–248.

Dienstbier, R. A. (1989). Arousal and physiological toughness: Implications for mental and physical health. *Psychological Review*, 96:84-100.

Dietary guidelines for Americans. (2005). Washington, DC: U. S. Department of Health and Human Services and U.S. Department of Agriculture.

Duke, N. K., & Pearson, P. D. (2001). Effective practices for developing reading comprehension. In *What Research Has to Say About Reading Instruction* (pp. 205–242). Ed. A. E. Farstrup and S. J. Samuels. Newark, DE: International Reading Association.

Dwyer, T., Sallis, J. F., Blizzard, L., Lazarus, R., & Dean, K. (2001). Relation of academic performance to physical activity and fitness in children. *Pediatric Exercise Science* (13): 225–238.

Ericsson, I. (2003). Motor skills, attention and academic achievements: An intervention study in school years 1–3. Ph.D. dis., Lunds Universitet, Sweden.

Florence, M. D., Asbridge, M., & Veugelers, P. J. (2008). Diet quality and academic performance. *Journal of School Health, 78*: 209–215.

Fogarty, R. (1991). Ten ways to integrate curriculum. *Educational Leadership, 49* (2): 61–65.

Gambrell, L., & Marniak, B. (1997). Incentives and intrinsic motivation to read. In *Reading Engagement: Motivating Readers Through Integrated Instruction*, ed. J. Guthrie and A. Wigfield, pp. 205–217. Newark, DE: International Reading Association.

Gardner, H. (1985). *Frames of mind: The theory of multiple intelligences*. New York: Basic Books.

Gavelek, J., Raphael, T., Biondo, S., & Wang, D. (2000). Integrated literacy instruction. In *Handbook of Reading Research, vol. 3*, ed. M. Kamil, P. Mosenthal, P. D. Pearson, and R. Barr, pp. 587–608. Mahwah, NJ: Lawrence Erlbaum.

Go, Slow, and Whoa Foods. (2005). Washington, DC: U.S. Department of Heart, Lung, and Blood Institute.

Goleman, D. (2006). *Social intelligence: The new science of human relationships*. New York: Bantam Dell.

Goleman, D. (1995). *Emotional intelligence*. New York: Bantam.

Graham, G., Holt/Hale, S. A., & Parker M. (2009). *Children moving: A reflective approach to teaching physical education* (8th ed.). New York: McGraw-Hill.

Guthrie, J., & Wigfield, A. (2000). Engagement and motivation in reading. In *Handbook of Reading Research*, Vol. 3, ed. M. Kamil, P. Mosenthal, P. D. Pearson, and R. Barr, pp. 403–422. Mahwah, NJ: Lawrence Erlbaum.

Guthrie, J. T. & McCann, A. D. (1996). Idea circles: Peer collaborations for conceptual learning." In L. B. Gambrell, and J. F. Almasi (eds). *Lively Discussions! Fostering Engaged Reading* (pp. 87–105). Newark, DE: International Reading Association.

Halliday, M. (1975). *Explorations in the functions of language*. London: Arnold.

Hannaford, C. (1995). *Smart moves: Why learning is not all in your head*. Arlington, VA: Great Ocean.

Harris, T., & Hodges, R. (1995). *The literacy dictionary: The vocabulary of reading and writing*. Newark, DE: International Reading Association.

Hastie, P., & Martin, E. (2006). *Teaching elementary physical education: Strategies for the classroom teacher*. New York: Pearson.

Heartaware: A heart healthy program. (2008). Fort Collins/Loveland, CO: Heart Center of the Rockies.

Hillman, C. H., Pontifex, M. B., Raine, L. B., Castelli, D. M., Hall, E. E., & Kramer, A. F. (2009).The effect of acute treadmill walking on cognitive control and academic achievement in preadolescent children. *Neuroscience, 159*: 1044–1054.

Hines, S. (2001). Physical fitness, academic achievement, and attitudes toward physical activity among fifth-grade elementary school students. Ph.D. dis., Northern Arizona University, Flagstaff, AZ.

Howard, P. (2000). *The owner's manual for the brain*. Austin, TX: Bard.

Jensen, E. (2006). *Enriching the brain: How to maximize every learner's potential*. San Francisco, CA: Jossey-Bass.

Jensen, E. (2000). *Brain-based learning*. San Diego, CA: The Brain Store.

Jensen, E., & Dabney, M. (2000). *Learning smarter*. San Diego, CA: The Brain Store.

Jones, S. (2006). *Girls, social class and literacy: What teachers can do to make a difference*. Portsmouth, NH: Heinemann.

Kohn, A. (1999). *Punished by rewards*. New York: Houghton Mifflin.

Kohn, A. (1992). *No contest: The case against competition* (revised ed.). New York: Houghton Mifflin.

Lasala, D. (1993). The relationship between physical fitness and academic achievement among urban middle school students. Ph.D. dis., Southern Connecticut State University, Storrs, CT.

Manzo, A.V. (1975). Guided reading procedure. *Journal of Reading, 18*: 287–291.

Marlett, P., & Gordon, C. (2004). The use of alternative texts in physical education. *Journal of Adolescent and Adult Literacy, 48* (3): 226–237.

Maslow, A. H. (1970). *Motivation and personality, 2nd ed.* New York: Harper & Row.

McLaughlin, M., & DeVoogd, G. (2004). Critical literacy as comprehension: Expanding reader response. *Journal of Adolescent and Adult Literacy, 43*: 52–62.

Mears, B. (2003). The ABCs of effective reading integration prek through first grade. *Teaching Elementary Physical Education, 14* (5): 36–39.

National Association of School Psychologists. (2008). Appropriate behavioral, social, and emotional supports to meet the needs of all students (position statement). Bethesda, MD.

Pittleman, S., Heimlich, J., Berglund, R., & French, M. (1991). *Semantic feature analysis: Classroom applications*. Newark, DE: International Reading Association.

President's Challenge: Physical Activity and Fitness Award Program. (2004). President's Council on Physical Fitness and Sports: U.S. Department of Health and Human Services.

Ratey, J. (with E. Hagerman). (2008). SPARK: The revolutionary new science of exercise and the brain. New York: Little, Brown.

Ready to learn, empowered to teach: Guiding principles for effective instruction. (2008). Bethesda, MD: National Association of School Psychologists (NASP).

Rosenblatt, L. (2002). The transactional theory of reading and writing. In R. B. Rudell and N. K. Unrau (Eds). *Theoretical Models and Processes of Reading (5th ed.)*, pp. 1363–1398. Newark, DE: International Reading Association.

Ruzzo, K., & Sacco, M. A. (2004). *Significant studies for second grade*. Portsmouth, NH: Heinemann.

Sanford-Smith, K., & Hopper, T. (1996). Teaching the mind and body: Connecting physical education and language arts. *Runner, 34* (1): 12–13.

Satcher, D. (2008). School wellness and the imperative of leadership. In *Progress or Promises? What's Working for and Against Healthy Schools: An Action for Healthy Kids Report* (pp. 8–10). Skokie, IL: Action for Healthy Kids.

Saul, W., J., Reardon, C., Pearce, D., Dieckman, & Neutze, D. (2002). *Science workshop: Reading, writing, and thinking like a scientist*. Portsmouth, NH: Heinemann.

Siegel, M. (2000). Word walls. *Teaching Elementary Physical Education, 11* (6): 11–12.

Stevens-Smith, D. (1999). Physical education in the classroom . . . You've got to be kidding! *Teaching Elementary Physical Education, 10* (1): 18–20.

Strauss, R. D., Rodzilsky, G., Burack, & Colin, M. (2001). Psychosocial correlates of physical activity in healthy children. *Archives of Pediatric Adolescent Medicine, 155*: 897–902.

Summerford, C. (2001). What is the impact of exercise on brain function for academic learning? *Teaching Elementary Physical Education, 12* (3): 6–8.

Taba, H. (1967). *Teacher's handbook for elementary social studies*. Reading, MA: Addison-Wesley.

The learning compact redefined: A call to action. *A Report of the Commission on the Whole Child*. (2007). Alexandria, VA: Association for the Supervision and Curriculum Development (ASCD).

Tyre, P. (2008). *The trouble with boys*. New York: Crown.

United States Department of Agriculture. (2005). *MyPyramid for Kids*.

United States Department of Health and Human Services. Centers for Disease Control. Retrieved 2/21/09 from http://www.education.com/partner/articles/cdc/.

United States Department of Health and Human Services. (2008). *2008 Physical Activity Guidelines for Americans*.

Vacca, R., & Vacca, J. (2008). *Content area reading: Literacy and learning across the curriculum, 8th ed*. New York: Allyn & Bacon.

Washington, R. (2009). Broadcast on childhood obesity. Retrieved from Colorado Public Radio on February 19, 2009.

Wahlstrom, K., & Begalle, M. (1999). More than test scores: Results of the universal school breakfast pilot in Minnesota. *Topics in Clinical Nutrition, 15* (1): 17–29.

Waite-Stupiansky, S., & Findlay, M. (2001). The fourth r: Recess and its link to learning. *Educational Forum, 66* (1): 16–24.

Wechsler, H., McKenna, M. L., Lee, S. M., & Dietz, W. H. (2004). The role of schools in preventing childhood obesity. *The State Education Standard* (December): 4–12.

Welk, G. J., & Blair, S. N. (2000). Physical activity protects against health risks of obesity. *President's Council on Physical Fitness and Sports Research Digest, 3*.

Whitin, D., & Wilde, S. (1995). *It's the story that counts: More children's books for mathematical learning, K–6*. Portsmouth, NH: Heinemann.

Wood, K., Lapp, D., Flood, J., & Taylor, D. B. (2008). *Guiding readers through text: Strategy guides for new times (2nd ed.)*. Newark, DE: International Reading Association.

Worrell, V., Kovar, S., & Oldfather, S. (2003). Brain/body connection as it relates to physical education. *Teaching Elementary Physical Education, 14* (6): 12–13, 26. *A Guide to Personal Fitness Training*. (2003). Sherman Oaks, CA: Aerobics and Fitness Association of America (AFFA).

Children's Literature Cited in Chapter Openers and Lesson Scenarios

Ashman, L. (2008). *M is for mischief: An a to z of naughty children*. New York: Dutton.

Cuyler, M. (2007). *Kindness is cooler, Mrs. Ruler*. New York: Simon & Schuster.

Elliott, D. (2009). *And here's to you*. Somerville, MA: Candlewick.

Ewald, W. (2002). *The best part of me: Children talk about their bodies in pictures and words*. New York: Little, Brown.

Foley, G. (2009). *Willoughby and the lion*. New York: Brown.

Guber, T., & Kalish, L. (2005). *Yoga pretzels*. Cambridge, MA: Barefoot Books.

Leedy, L. (2007). *The edible pyramid: Good eating every day (revised ed.)*. New York: Holiday House.

McCarthy, M. (2007). *Strong man: The story of Charles Atlas*. New York: Knopf.

Miller, E. (2006). *The monster health book*. New York: Holiday House.

Parker, S. (2003). *100 things you should know about the human body*. New York: Barnes and Noble.

Rosenthal, A. K. (2007). *The OK book*. New York: HarperCollins.

Roy, J. (2009). *Max Quigley: Technically NOT a bully*. New York: Houghton Mifflin.

Shannon, G. (1997). *True lies: 18 tales for you to judge*. New York: HarperCollins.

Simon, S. (1998). *Muscles: Our muscular system*. New York: Morrow.

Tibo, G. (2002). *Shy guy*. New York: North-South.

Weeks, S. (2003). *Two eggs, please*. New York: Atheneum.

Williams, R. (2008). *Human anatomy*. San Francisco: File Mile Press.

Wolf, A. (2003). *The blood-hungry spleen and other poems about our parts*. Cambridge, MA: Candlewick.

Zalben, J. B. (2006). *Paths to peace: People who changed the world*. New York: Dutton.

Ziefert, H. (2003). *You can't see your bones with binoculars: A guide to your 206 bones*. Maplewood, NJ: Blue Apple.

Appendix A

Additional FitLit Titles

Physical Fitness

Berry, L. (2008). *Duck dunks*. New York: Henry Holt and Company.

Branner, T. (2007). *Care and feeding of an athlete: What you need to know to rise to the top of your game*. Saint Augustine, FL: Blue Water Press.

Creaemer, M. B. (2006). *Coco loves to tri*. Upton, MA: Power Pack Presentations.

Cronin, D., & Menchin, S. (2007). *Bounce*. New York: Atheneum Books for Young Readers.

Cronin, D. (2009) *Stretch*. New York: Atheneum Books for Young Readers.

Davids, T. (2009). *Wrestling the ABCs: Creating character and fostering fitness*. Northville, MI: Ferne Press.

Falwell, C. (2008). *Scoot!* New York: Greenwillow Books.

Fehler, G. (2009). *Change-up: Baseball poems*. New York: Clarion Books.

Goodrow, C. (2008). *Kids running: Have fun, get faster and go farther*. Halcottsville, NY: Breakaway Books.

Goodrow, C. (2006). *The treasure of health and happiness*. Halcottsville, NY: Breakaway Books.

Hallinan, P.K. (2007). *Let's be fit*. Nashville: Ideals Children's Books.

Isadora, R. (2001). *Nick plays baseball*. New York: G. P. Putnam's Sons.

Katz, A. (2009). *Going, going, gone! And other silly dilly sports*. New York: Margaret K. McElderry Books.

Lowery, L. (1995). *Twist with a burger, jitter with a bug*. Boston: Houghton Mifflin.

Maloney, P. (2000). *Belly button boy*. New York: Puffin Books.

Morrison, T. (2009). *Peeny butter fudge*. New York: Simon & Schuster.

O'Connor, J. (2007). *Ready, set, skip!* New York: Penguin Books.

Parker, N. W. (2009). *Organs! How they work, fall apart, and can be replaced (gasp!)*. New York: Greenwillow Books.

Parker, V. (1999). *Bearobics*. New York: Puffin Books.

Rabe, T. (2001). *Oh the things you can do that are good for you!* New York: Random House Books for Young Readers.

Rau, D.M. (2009). *Fitness for fun!* Minneapolis, MN: Compass Point Books.

Rex, M. (2005). *Dunk skunk*. New York: G. P. Putnam's Sons.

Rosen, M., & Oxenbury, H. (2007). *We're going on a bear hunt: A celebratory pop-up edition*. New York: Little Simon.

Royston, A. (2004). *My amazing body: Moving*. Eustis, FL: Raintree.

Seder, R. B. (2008). *Swing!* New York: Workman Publishing Company.

Showers, P. (1997). *Sleep is for everyone*. New York: HarperCollins Children's Books.

Shulman, L. (2007). *Over in the meadow at the big ballet*. New York: G. P. Putnam's Sons.

Smith, C.R. (2008). *Short takes*. New York: Dutton Children's Books.

Taylor, S. (2005). *Boing!* New York: Walker Books.

Thomas, J. (2009). *Can you make a scary face?* New York: Beach Lane Books.

Yelenak, A. (2004). *Run, dad, run!* Halcottsville, NY: Breakaway Books.

Nutritional Fitness

Barron, R. (2000). *Fed up! A feast of frazzled foods*. New York: G. P. Putnam's Sons.

Barron, R. (2004). *Showdown at the food pyramid*. New York: G. P. Putnam's Sons.

Burns, M. (1997). *Spaghetti and meatballs for all! A mathematics story*. New York: Scholastic.

Carle, E. (1990). *Pancakes, pancakes!* New York: Scholastic.

Child, L. (2000). *I will never not eat a tomato*. Somerville, MA: Candlewick Press.

Deen, P. (2009). *Paula Deen's cookbook for the lunch-box set*. New York: Simon & Schuster.

Derby, S. (2008). *No mush today!* New York: Lee & Low Books.

Durand, H. (2009). *Dessert first*. New York: Atheneum Books for Young Readers.

Evans, C. (2008). *Bone soup*. Boston: Houghton Mifflin Company.

Haduch, B. (2001). *Food rules: The stuff you munch, its crunch, its punch, and why you sometimes lose your lunch*. New York: Dutton Children's Books.

Hewitt, S. (2005). *Health and diet: Looking after myself*. Mankato, MN: Stargazer Books.

Kasza, K. (2007). *Badger's fancy meal*. New York: Puffin Books.

Kleven, E. (2001). *Sun bread*. New York: Puffin Books.

Krull, K. (2001). *Supermarket*. New York: Holiday House.

Lindsey, K. D. (2003). *Sweet potato pie*. New York: Lee & Low Books.

Mathers, P. (2000). *A cake for Herbie*. New York: Atheneum Books for Young Readers.

McDonald, M. (2005). *Beetle McGrady eats bugs!* New York: Greenwillow Books.

Miller, E. (2006). *The monster health group: A guide to eating healthy, being active, and feeling great for monsters and kids!* New York: Holiday House.

Munsch, R. (2002). *More pies!* New York: Cartwheel Books.

Robbins, K. (2005). *Seeds*. New York: Atheneum Books for Young Readers.

Rubel, N. (2002). *No more vegetables*. New York: Farrar, Straus & Giroux.

Sharmat, M. (1989). *Gregory, the terrible eater*. New York: Scholastic.

Shryer, D. (2007). *Body fuel: A guide to good nutrition*. Tarrytown, NY: Marshall Cavendish Children's Books.

Solheim, J. (1998). *It's disgusting . . . and we ate it! True food facts from around the world and throughout history*. New York: Simon & Schuster.

Stern. S. (2008). *Sam Stern's real food, real fast*. Somerville, MA: Candlewick Press.

Tolstoy, A. (1998). *The gigantic turnip*. Cambridge, MA: Barefoot Books.

Weeks, S. (2003). *Two eggs, please*. New York: Atheneum Books for Young Readers.

Winkler, P. (2002). *Keeping fit*. Washington, D.C.: National Geographic Society.

Social Fitness

Anderson, L.H. (2009). *Wintergirls*. New York: Viking Children's Books.

Ashman, L. (2008). *M is for mischief*. New York: Dutton Children's Books.

Barber, R., Barber, T., & Burleigh, R. (2005). *Game day*. New York: Simon & Schuster.

Barber, R., Barber, T., & Burleigh, R. (2006). *Teammates*. New York: Simon & Schuster.

Bardhan-Quallen, S. (2007). *Mine-o-saur*. New York: Scholastic.

Bildner, P. (2006). *The greatest game ever played*. New York: G. P. Putnam's Sons.

Bildner, P. (2002). *Shoeless Joe and Black Betsy*. New York: Simon & Schuster.

Bildner, P. (2005). *The shot heard 'round the world*. New York: Simon & Schuster.

Christie, R. G. (2009). *Make way for Dyamonde Daniel*. New York: G. P. Putnam's Sons.

Cooper, F. (2008). *Willie and the all-stars*. New York: Philomel Books.

Cooper, I. (2007). *The golden rule*. New York: Abrams Books for Young Readers.

Criswell, P. K. (2004). *What would you do? Quizzes about real-life problems*. Middleton, WI: American Girl Publishing.

Cuyler, M. (2007). *Kindness is cooler, Mrs. Ruler*. New York: Simon & Schuster.

Dempsey, K. (2009). *Me with you*. New York: Philomel Books.

Driscoll, L. (2002). *The Negro Leagues: All black baseball*. New York: Grosset & Dunlap.

Elya-Middleton, S. (2002). *Eight animals bake a cake*. New York: G. P. Putnam's Sons.

Foreman, M. (2002). *Wonder goal!* New York: Farrar, Straus & Giroux.

Friedman, D. (2009). *Star of the week: A story of love, adoption, and brownies with sprinkles*. New York: Bowen Press.

Galen, A. (2009). *Billy Bully: A schoolyard counting tale*. New York: Scholastic.

Gorbachev, V. (2009). *Molly who flew away*. New York: Philomel Books.

Green, T. (2007). *Football genius*. New York: HarperCollins Publishers.

Greenfield, E. (2009). *Brothers and sisters: Family poems*. New York: Amistad.

Holmes, E. (2009). *Tracktown summer*. New York: Dutton Children's Books.

Isadora, R. (2009). *The ugly duckling*. New York: G. P. Putnam's Sons.

Keller, L. (2007). *Do unto otters: A book about manners*. New York: Scholastic.

Lasky, K. (2009). *Poodle and hound*. Watertown, MA: Charlesbridge.

Lerman, J. (2009). *How to raise mom and dad*. New York: Dutton Children's Books..

Loribiecki, M. (2006). *Jackie's bat*. New York: Simon & Schuster.

Lupica, M. (2007). *Two-minute drill: A comeback kids novel*. New York: Philomel Books.

Lyon, G. E. (2009). *You and me and home sweet home*. New York: Atheneum Books for Young Readers.

Maloney, P. (1999). *The magic hockey stick*. New York: Puffin Books.

McGuirk, L., & Von Bidder, A. (2009). *Wiggins learns his manners at the Four Seasons Restaurant*. Somerville, MA: Candlewick Press.

McKissack, P. C. (2008). *The home run king*. New York: Viking Press.

Mora, P. (2009). *Gracias, thanks*. New York: Lee & Low Books.

Nickle, J. (1999). *The ant bully*. New York: Scholastic.

Numeroff, L. (2009). *What sisters do best, what brothers do best*. San Francisco: Chronicle Books.

Post, P., and Senning, C. P. (2009). *Emily Post's table manners for kids*. New York: Collins.

Potter, E. (2009). *Slob*. New York: Philomel Books.

Primavera, E. (2009). *Louis the big cheese*. New York: Simon & Schuster.

Robbins, J. (2009). *Two of a kind*. New York: Atheneum Books for Young Readers.

Scanlon, L. G. (2009). *All the world*. New York: Beach Lane.

Schindel, J. (2003). *What did they see?* New York: Henry Holt & Company.

Scieszka, J. (2008). *Smash! Crash!* New York: Simon & Schuster.

Segal, J. (2006). *Carrot soup*. New York: Margaret K. McElderry Books.

Sones, S., & Tramer, B. (2009). *Violet and Winston*. New York: Dial Books.

Stein, D. E. (2008). *The nice book*. New York: G.P. Putnam's Sons.

Stevens, J. (1999). *Cock-a-doodle-doo!* New York: Harcourt Brace & Company.

Stevens, J. (2008). *Help me, Mr. Mutt!* New York: Harcourt Brace & Company.

Tavares, M. (2004). *Oliver's game*. Somerville, MA: Candlewick Press.

Tavares, M. (2000). *Zachary's ball*. Somerville, MA: Candlewick Press.

Warburg, S. S. (1993). *I like you*. Boston: Houghton Mifflin.

Weatherford, C. B. (2005). *A Negro League scrapbook*. Honesdale, PA: Boyds Mills Press.

Wing, N. (1996). *Jalapeño bagels*. New York: Atheneum Books for Young Readers.

Winters, K. (2002). *But mom, everybody else does*. New York: Dutton Children's Books.

Wolff, N. (2005). *Tallulah in the kitchen*. New York: Henry Holt and Company.

Yep, L. (2008). *Dragon road*. New York: HarperCollins Children's Books.

Emotional Fitness

Adler, D. A. (1997). *Lou Gehrig: The luckiest man*. Orlando, FL: Voyager Books.

Bardhan-Quallen, S. (2006). *Tightrope Poppy, the high-wire pig*. New York: Sterling Publishing.

Beaumont, K. (2004). *I like myself!* Orlando, FL: Harcourt.

Brisson, P. (2006). *Melissa Parkington's beautiful, beautiful hair*. Honesdale, PA: Boyds Mills Press.

Brown, M. (2009). *Pele: King of soccer*. New York: HarperCollins Publishers.

Bruel, N. (2006). *Who is Melvin Bubble?* New York: Roaring Brook Press.

Carlson, N. (2009). *I like me!* New York: Puffin Books.

Carlson, N. (2002). *Smile a lot!* Minneapolis, MN: Carolrhoda Books.

Child, L. (2009). *I will be especially very careful*. New York: Dial Books.

Cochran, B. (2009). *My parents are divorced, my elbows have nicknames, and other facts about me*. New York: HarperCollins Publishers.

Covey, S. (2009). *The seven habits of happy kids*. New York: Simon & Schuster.

Crow, K. (2009). *The middle-child blues*. New York: G. P. Putnam's Sons.

Cuyler, M. (2009). *Bullies never win*. New York: Simon & Schuster.

Dewdney, A. (2009). *Llama llama, mad at mama*. New York: Viking Children's Books.

Dewdney, A. (2009). *Llama llama, misses mama*. New York: Viking Children's Books.

Elffers, J. (2009). *Do you love me?* New York: Bowen Press.

Elliott, D. (2004). *And here's to you!* Somerville, MA: Candlewick Press.

Elliott, Z. (2008). *Bird*. New York: Lee & Low Books.

Falconer, I. (2009). *Olivia*. New York: Atheneum. Books for Young Readers

George, M. (2009). *Looks*. New York: Speak.

Greenfield, E. (2009). *Paul Robeson*. New York: Lee & Low.

Hicks, B. (2009). *Track attack*. New York: Roaring Brook Press.

Hillenbrand, W. (2009). *Louie!* New York: Philomel Books.

Jordan, D., & Jordan, R. (2007). *Michael's golden rules*. New York: Paula Wiseman Books.

Juster, N. (2008). *Sourpuss and Sweetie Pie*. New York: Scholastic.

Keane, D. (2009). *Sloppy Joe*. New York: HarperCollins Publishers.

Lester, H. (2003). *Something might happen*. Boston: Houghton Mifflin.

Levy, E. (2005). *Tackling dad*. New York: HarperCollins Publishers.

Lionni, L. (1992). *Tico and the golden wings*. New York: Alfred A. Knopf Books.

McCarthy, M. (2007). *Strong man: The story of Charles Atlas*. New York: Alfred A. Knopf Books.

McEvoy, A. (2009). *Betsy B. Little*. New York: HarperCollins Publishers.

Milford, S. (2007). *Pebble: A story about belonging*. New York: HarperCollins Publishers.

Nikola-Lisa, W. (2009). *How smart we are*. New York: Lee & Low.

Paley, S. (2007). *Huge*. New York: Simon Pulse.

Parton, D. (2009). *I am a rainbow*. New York: G. P. Putnam's Sons.

Patron, S. (2006). *The higher power of lucky*. New York: Aladdin Books.

Paul, C. (2009). *Long shot*. New York: Simon & Schuster.

Piven, H. (2006). *What athletes are made of*. New York: Atheneum Books for Young Readers.

Posada, J., & Burleigh, R. (2006). *Play ball!* New York: Simon & Schuster.

Postgate, D. (2009). *The snaggle grollop*. New York: Scholastic.

Reynolds, P. H. (2009). *The north star*. Somerville, MA: Candlewick Press.

Richardson, C. K. (2005). *The real lucky charm*. New York: Dial Books for Young Readers.

Literacy Lessons to Help Kids Get Fit & Healthy

Riggio, A. (2002). *Smack dab in the middle*. New York: G. P. Putnam's Sons.

Robberecht, T. (2004). *Angry dragon*. New York: Clarion Books.

Rosen, M. (2009). *I'm number one*. Somerville, MA: Candlewick Press.

Rosenthal, A.K., & Lichtenheld, T. (2007). *The OK book*. New York: HarperCollins Publishers.

Rosenthal, A. K. (2006). *One of those days*. New York: Putnam Juvenile.

Schroeder, A. (2009). *In her hands: The story of sculptor Augusta Savage*. New York: Lee & Low.

Scotton, R. (2008). *Love, splat*. New York: HarperCollins Publishers.

Segal, J. (2009). *Far far away!* New York: Philomel Books.

Spinelli, E. (2006). *When you are happy*. New York: Simon & Schuster.

Tavares, M. (2005). *Mudball*. Somerville, MA: Candlewick Press.

Torrey, R. (2009). *Almost*. New York: HarperCollins Publishers.

Vail, R. (2005). *Sometimes I'm a Bombaloo*. New York: Scholastic.

Vaughan, M. (2003). *Up the learning tree*. New York: Lee & Low.

Weeks, S. (2009). *Catfish Kate and the Sweet Swamp Band*. New York: Atheneum Books for Young Readers.

Wilson, K. (2009). *Don't be afraid, Little Pip*. New York: Simon & Schuster.

Yoo, P. (2009). *Shining star: The Anna May Wong story*. New York: Lee & Low.

A Close Look at MyPyramid *For Kids*

MyPyramid for Kids reminds you to be physically active every day, or most days, and to make healthy food choices. Every part of the new symbol has a message for you. Can you figure it out?

Be Physically Active Every Day

The person climbing the stairs reminds you to do something active every day, like running, walking the dog, playing, swimming, biking, or climbing lots of stairs.

Eat More From Some Food Groups Than Others

Did you notice that some of the color stripes are wider than others? The different sizes remind you to choose more foods from the food groups with the widest stripes.

Choose Healthier Foods From Each Group

Why are the colored stripes wider at the bottom of the pyramid? Every food group has foods that you should eat more often than others; these foods are at the bottom of the pyramid.

Every Color Every Day

The colors orange, green, red, yellow, blue, and purple represent the five different food groups plus oils. Remember to eat foods from all food groups every day.

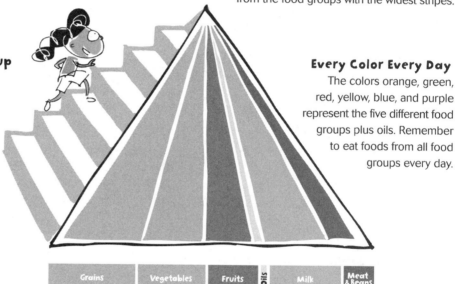

Grains | Vegetables | Fruits | Oils | Milk | Meat & Beans

Make Choices That Are Right for You

MyPyramid.gov is a Web site that will give everyone in the family personal ideas on how to eat better and exercise more.

Take One Step at a Time

You do not need to change overnight what you eat and how you exercise. Just start with one new, good thing, and add a new one every day.

MyPyramid.gov
STEPS TO A HEALTHIER YOU

U.S. Department of Agriculture
Food and Nutrition Service
September 2005
FNS-388

USDA is an equal opportunity provider and employer.

USDA

TEAM NUTRITION
teamnutrition.usda.gov

MyPyramid Worksheet

Name: _____

Check how you did yesterday and set a goal to aim for tomorrow

Write In Your Choices From Yesterday	Food and Activity	Tip	Goal (Based On a 1800 Calorie Pattern)	List Each Food Choice In Its Food Group*	Estimate Your Total
Breakfast:	**Grains**	Make at least half your grains whole grains.	**6 ounce equivalents** (1 ounce equivalent is about 1 slice bread, 1 cup dry cereal, or ½ cup cooked rice, pasta, or cereal)		____ ounce equivalents
Lunch:	**Vegetables**	Color your plate with all kinds of great tasting veggies.	**2½ cups** (Choose from dark green, orange, starchy, dry beans and peas, or other veggies).		____ cups
Snack:	**Fruits**	Make most choices fruit, not juice.	**1½ cups**		____ cups
Dinner:	**Milk**	Choose fat-free or lowfat most often.	**3 cups** (1 cup yogurt or 1½ ounces cheese = 1 cup milk)		____ cups
	Meat and Beans	Choose lean meat and chicken or turkey. Vary your choices—more fish, beans, peas, nuts, and seeds.	**5 ounce equivalents** (1 ounce equivalent is 1 ounce meat, chicken or turkey, or fish, 1 egg, 1 T. peanut butter, ½ ounce nuts, or ¼ cup dry beans)		____ ounce equivalents
Physical activity:	**Physical Activity**	Build more physical activity into your daily routine at home and school.	At least **60 minutes** of moderate to vigorous activity a day or most days.		____ minutes

* Some foods don't fit into any group. These "extras" may be mainly fat or sugar—limit your intake of these.

How did you do yesterday?   ☐ Great   ☐ So-So   ☐ Not So Great

My food goal for tomorrow is: _____

My activity goal for tomorrow is: _____

U R What U Eat

Food supplies the nutrients needed to fuel your body so you can perform your best. Go, Slow, Whoa is a simple way to recognize foods that are the smartest choices.
- **"Go"** Foods: Eat almost anytime (Most often) — they are lowest in fat, added sugar, and calories
- **"Slow"** Foods: Eat sometimes (Less often) — they are higher in fat, added sugar, and/or calories
- **"Whoa"** Foods: Eat once in a while (Least often) — they are very high in fat and/or added sugar, and are much higher in calories

Food Groups	GO	SLOW	WHOA
Fruits Whole fruits (fresh, frozen, canned, dried) are smart choices. You need **2 cups** of fruit a day. 1 cup is about the size of a baseball.			
Vegetables Adding fat (butter, oils, and sauces) to vegetables turns them from Go foods to Slow or Whoa foods. You need **2 ½ cups** of vegetables a day. Dark green and orange vegetables are smart choices.			
Grains Try to make at least half of your servings whole grain choices and low in sugar. An ounce of a grain product is 1 slice of bread, 1 cup of dry cereal, or ½ cup of cooked rice or pasta. You need about **6 ounces** a day.			
Milk Milk products are high in vitamins and minerals. Fat-free and low-fat milk and milk products are smart choices. About **3 cups** are needed each day; 1 cup of milk, 1 cup of yogurt or 1 ½ ounces of natural cheese count as 1 cup.			
Meats & Beans Eating **5 ½ oz.** a day will give you the protein, vitamins and minerals you need. Limit meats with added fat. Smart choices include beans (¼ cup cooked), nuts (½ oz.) and lean meats (1 oz.) baked or broiled.			

The amounts of foods recommended per food group are based on a 2,000-calorie diet, the approximate number of calories for most active boys and girls ages 9-13. U.S. Department of Agriculture, Center for Nutrition Policy and Promotion.

We can!
Ways to Enhance Children's Activity & Nutrition

NATIONAL INSTITUTES OF HEALTH